This is by far the best book ev   believe
us, read the reviews.

"The best book ever written in the history of the universe. I highly recommend buying at least 10 copies."
—Calvin Boyden Walker, Author
(Unless you are suing us) of this book

"My brother paid me three dollars to tell you this is the best book ever written."
—Alexandra Boyden Walker,
Sister of Calvin Boyden Walker

"This had better be the best book ever written in the history of the universe or you're grounded for life."
—Dad

The book is really great, it has hundreds of fun activities that you can do. Some of the ideas are free and only take a few minutes while others may cost a small fortune and take years. We have also included some useful ideas, such as creative ways to earn money and ideas to make your parents happy. We have added a number of activities you can do with your friends or to do to make new friends. The first section includes lists of activities that people can do, from cooking to earning money. The second includes things that kids should know about, like how to avoid being poor, how to negotiate, how to tell if someone is lying, and other similar skills. The third is similar to the second, only more focused on health. We realize that some of the sections are simply long lists so at the bottom we added "activities" which serve as hints or jumping off points for that particular list. In any case, it is a great book. Pick it up and read it when your parents ask what you are doing.

UNPLUGGED

Hundreds of Activities
for Teens to Do
Without a Screen

Paul Walker

Alexandra Boyden Walker

Calvin Boyden Walker

Robert D. Reed Publishers
www.rdrpublishers.com
Bandon, OR

ROBERT D. REED PUBLISHERS

Robert D. Reed Publishers
P.O. Box 1992
Bandon, OR 97411
Phone: 541-347-9882; Fax: -9883
E-mail: 4bobreed@msn.com
Website: www.rdrpublishers.com

Editor/Designer: Cleone Reed
Cover: Cleone Reed

Author photos: Isabella Cavallero, izzycavallero@gmail.com

Soft Cover ISBN: 978-1-944297-58-9
EBook ISBN: 978-1-944297-59-6

Library of Congress Control Number: 2020931226

Designed and Formatted in the United States of America

Dedication

This book is dedicated to
Mom, aka Genevieve Walker

Acknowledgments

First of all we would like to thank our Uncle Jerry, Jerry Walters, who showed us that we could rent a speed boat using our dad's charge card, despite the fact we do not have driver's licenses, and then attach our father to a rope and drag him across a lake at ungodly speeds while listening to him scream like a little girl. (Oops that's sexist—like a young lady.)

There are a few teachers who Alexandra thinks are particularly terrific. Two teachers from middle school that were especially great include Mr. Norwood and Ms. Eurgubian at San Jose Middle School who showed her what good teaching looks like and encouraged her to challenge herself. Her English Teacher at Marin Academy, Bijani Mizel, is also amazing, as well as her math teacher and water polo coach, Jamie Collie, who was especially helpful and supportive when she discovered water polo is not just volley ball in a wading pool. These teachers have really encouraged and challenged her. Thanks!

Calvin would like to thank Mr. Gersh in the Digital Arts Program and Ms. Kaleen in the Fine Arts program at Marin School of the Arts for encouraging him to be creative and Ms. Polluck who told him he should join her class as a student instead of just hanging out and drinking tea.

We also want to thank our mom for being the greatest mom ever and who we hope will decide as a reward for dedicating this book to her that she will never make us do any more chores.

Dad would also like to thank his children for writing his book and his two cats who have truly been an inspiration and great role models.

Contents

SECTION ONE:
FUN AND INTERESTING
ACTIVITIES WITHOUT A SCREEN
17

**SECTION TWO:
THINGS THEY DON'T TEACH YOU
IN SCHOOL BUT SHOULD
97**

SECTION THREE:
HOW TO BE HEALTHY, WEALTHY, AND WISE
111

A Note to Parents

Dear Parents (and legal guardians):

As a concerned child of the modern age, I can't help but fear for the mental health and future of my fellow youth in this hard, cruel world.

Children of my age see unbelievably egregious, indecorous, and obscene things on the internet. Unfortunately, it seems that there's virtually no way to prevent them from seeing these things. Oh, the problems of the poor, disadvantaged children of this time! Once, I endured the dreadful effort of using the internet (yes, the internet!) to research how much time teens spend on the computer. What I found was that average teens spend a shocking nine hours a day on social media, and only seventeen hours a week studying! How outrageously unfathomable! Personally, I spend over 22 hours per day engrossed in my studies. I recommend that other teenagers do the same.

For real though, think about it: we are the first generation to have an almost infinite amount of information literally at our fingertips. And yet, few young people actually use it to learn or think. Not only are they reading less, but the information they receive and regurgitate is often garbage.

I think most people are aware of the common pitfalls of the digital generation. But I also have another concern. If the average high-school student is spending nine hours a day on a device, then they are not doing other activities. Students who don't spend time with others will likely grow up with distorted social skills. Additionally, students who don't read or study will be far behind people like me, a student who spends many hours a day engaged in studies.

Sure, the internet allows you to connect with people online, but in many cases, this simply encourages bad behavior. If your online "friends" spend hours a day playing some game, you begin to think that spending that kind of time on gaming is normal. And who even knows who these "friends" are? They could be forty-year-old guys in their mom's basement trying to get a date, for all you know. Anyway, spending almost 136 days a year, in hours, on a device is most definitely a waste of a life.

—Calvin and Alexandra

A Note to Readers

Assuming people even read these nowadays, here's an explanation of the overall layout of this book. There are three sections. The first includes long lists of activities from sports to arts and crafts to hobbies and cooking. The second part includes things that you should know or be able to do but which are not taught in school. Thrown in are a few things that teenagers should probably know about themselves, courtesy of the Old Man. The third section is focused on how to be healthy, wealthy, and wise, a title that is pretty self-explanatory.

We realize that some of the sections are simply long lists so at the bottom we have added "activities" which serve as hints or jumping off points for that particular list.

Occasionally you'll see the heading "Alternatively", indicating a different approach that can be taken to that activity. Be warned though, they're usually a bit saucy.

At the end of the book, we ask for your suggestions, comments, and feedback. In case you're a parent who might complain that the book is not complete, or that we are politically incorrect, we use he/she/him/her/they and them.

PESSIMISM WARNING: The following contains some of the most pessimistic optimism I've ever read. You have been warned.

CONTROVERSY WARNING: My Dear Old Man has no filter. Of course, keep in mind that anything in the final version has been severely toned down since previous drafts. Still, I will attach the tag,

"Incoming Dad Rant" when one is about to appear. Additionally, there will be a number of x's after the warning, ranging from zero to however many I feel is necessary to get the point across. Here's a chart that may be helpful.

—	Rare (Run-of-the-mill Dad Rant.)
X	Medium-rare Controversy
XX	Medium Controversy
XXX	Medium-well Controversy/Insensitivity
XXXX	Toasty Controversy/Insensitivity (Might want to skip this.)
XXXXX	Scorching Controversy/Insensitivity (We probably shouldn't have included this.)
XXXXX+	Hellfire (Dad wouldn't let us cut it…)
XXXXX++	Really Bad

ONE

FUN AND INTERESTING ACTIVITIES WITHOUT A SCREEN

0

Technically Not an Activity; End Climate Change in 12 Months or Less

INCOMING DAD RANT— CONTROVERSY SCORE XX

If you want to reduce greenhouse gases, you could buy a $100,000 electric car that basically burns coal. But if you drive that car to the grocery store and buy a pound of hamburger meat, you've gone and wasted that $100,000. The fact is, 45% of greenhouse pollution, specifically methane, comes from cows, an amount higher than the amount from cars, planes, trucks, trains, and boats combined.

The solution is simple. Kill all the cows. Now, I know what you're thinking. Wouldn't that create a black market for cow? Not what you were thinking? Ah well, I'll answer it anyway. People love to eat dead animals, so say people simply created a black market for cows. The answer to that is to make the penalty for selling cow parts five years in prison. This would discourage most people from raising and selling cows. The added advantage is that the drug cartels could switch from selling crack, heroin, and marijuana to children to selling hotdogs to them. It's a win-win situation.

Okay, so now let's address what you're probably actually thinking. I'm guessing it's something along the lines of, "Killing all the cows? That's outrageous/terrible/could never happen," so here's a more reasonable solution: tax cows instead. The average American consumes around 220 pounds of beef a year. There are roughly 325 million people, so the total pounds of beef eaten is 5.5 billion pounds of beef. If you tax beef at one dollar a pound, you will have 5.5 billion dollars to fight the effects of climate change.

Now, you may be wondering why we chose to start a book on activities for teens with climate change. There are four reasons, the second of which has been rated Incoming Dad Rant XXX. (You've been warned!) First and foremost, it's to show you that you can change the world. I really do believe this, but in order to do so we need to understand the complexity of the world. Most politicians and social justice advocates regurgitate slogans and rhetoric in a way to invoke our emotions, which is condescending and counterproductive. Just because something sounds good or riles up your emotions doesn't mean it's the truth, or a good solution, and understanding that the world isn't as simple as people make it out to be is an excellent starting point for finding solutions that work.

WARNING: INCOMING DAD RANT— CONTROVERSY SCORE XXX

The second reason we started with climate change is to point out that old people hate you. While they have been called "the Greatest Generation", they were in fact the most selfish and idiotic generation in the history of humankind, who have left the nation with a trillion dollar debt and over 100 trillion in unfunded mandates, which are to be paid for by their kids, grandkids, and your kids. Not only did they promise to give themselves ridiculous benefits, but they also spent the money to pay for these benefits on other things such as, the F-35 fighter jet, which is 175 billion over budget, and $325,000 for 391 coffee cups for the Air Force. Despite the fact that the country is already well beyond broke, they just keep on spending. And every election year politicians promise more and more stuff, like free college for crackheads and free healthcare for cigarette smokers. They sound like six-year-old children crying that the world is unfair so we should give everyone a balloon and college education for free.

INCOMING DAD RANT— CONTROVERSY SCORE X

The third reason for starting with climate change is to start to think about how you want to make a difference. The truth is, you can make a huge difference by taking relatively small actions. A dwarf apple tree produces between 375 and 750 apples a year. Plant two apple trees at your school and you could grow up to 1,500 free apples a year. There are over 130,000 schools in the United States and if each school had two apple trees, well, you'd have a lot of apples.

But if you don't care that the earth is heating or cooling or changing, then find something else you would like to change, improve, or fix and start working on finding and implementing a solution.

ACTIVITIES

- Think about the things you would like to improve or change. If you are concerned about the environment, is there something you could do to help that you would enjoy doing?

- Come up with a few simple things you could do to make the world a better place, such as planting a tree or baking cookies for your classmates.

- As you are reading the book, think about how you can combine things you like to do with activities that will help you or help others. If you love being social, maybe you can organize a party that raises money for one of your favorite causes, or if you love animals you can volunteer at an animal shelter.

1

Start a Journal

WARNING: INCOMING DAD RANT— CONTROVERSY SCORE X

We should look at becoming an optimist. This isn't easy. Unless you live under a rock, you will have heard that the world is in a mess. The polar ice caps are melting, the president is a nut (no matter who's in office when you're reading this, someone's going to think so), and most likely the next president will also be a nut. Our schools are crumbling; people are mad about everything from which sex can use which bathroom to whether wearing a Hawaiian shirt is cultural appropriation. Still, it's important to remember the good too, which is why it could be an excellent idea to start an "Attitude of Gratitude" journal, where every day you write down good things.

Yes, the world has problems, huge problems, and things are not improving. Fifty years ago, the president of the United States called two astronauts while they were on the moon. Last year, Trump invited Kim Kardashian to the White House. And yes, there are more greenhouse gases in the atmosphere than ever before, but the greenhouse gas carbon dioxide is beneficial to plants as is the other greenhouse gas, water. (Yes, water vapor is considered a greenhouse gas.)

Things seem worse in part because social media bombards us with images of family, friends, and complete strangers who all seem to be fantastic looking while doing fantastic things. Nobody posts pictures of cutting themselves shaving, going to the dentist, or doing their laundry. (Okay maybe they do, but they only show the perfect shave, the fabulous dentist, and their best laundry.)

ACTIVITIES

- Start a Gratitude Journal and each day list three things you are grateful for.

- Keep a journal where you write how you can change your attitude.

- Learn how to change the questions you ask. Our brains always give us a fast answer, so why not learn to ask better questions. Instead of asking the question, "Why am I doing poorly in math?" ask, "How can I get an "A" in math?" Instead of, "Why am I out of shape?" ask, "How can I get into shape?"

- Set goals. Create plans and look

ALTERNATIVELY

Start a hate journal, where you write about the things that drive you crazy or make you mad. Then burn it. It's very liberating, and even if you don't have access to say, a fire pit, tearing it up and throwing it away can feel almost as good. I think there's probably supposed to be some deep message about throwing away the bad or something, but honestly it can feel nice to just get it all out.

2

Art and Creative Projects

ART PROJECTS

Art projects are a classic activity, so there are plenty of art projects you can do. I have compiled a few below for varying skill levels. Some of these are easy; you don't need any skill or training at all! Others are more complicated or require special equipment. Even if you are not great at art, you can still do tons of fun art projects; many of these are projects even Dad can do.

BEGINNING PROJECTS

- Take photographs.
- Create a photograph album.
- Turn your photographs into a shirt design.
- Take selfies with someone else.
- Make a slideshow with a bunch of photographs for your parents or friends.
- Take a photography class.
- Try collage.

- Create a scrapbook.
- Create a mural with bottle caps.
- Learn the art of floral arrangement.
- Use nature to make art. (Ow! My eye!)
- Make art with food.
- Paint by numbers.
- Art supplies can be pricey, but not to make these art projects!
- Learn to draw.
- Sketch.
- Draw a landscape.
- Draw an imaginary place.
- Draw your pet.
- Chalk art.
- Draw with pencils.
- Draw with crayons.
- Draw cartoons.

OTHER BEGINNER ART PROJECTS COULD INCLUDE

- Paint.
- Paint with oils.
- Paint your furniture.
- Make prints.
- Learn to sculpt.
- Create with clay.
- Create with Sculpey.
- Make a Lego sculpture.
- Make ceramics.

- Design dishes.
- Put art on dishes.
- Make things with *papier-mâché* (yes, there are more things you can make than volcanoes).
- Make a mask.
- Learn calligraphy (with those really cool pens).
- Try decoupage.

OTHER CREATIVE ACTIVITIES COULD INCLUDE

- Learn how to edit films.
- Create a holiday movie instead of a card.
- Create a graphic novel.
- Create animated cartoons.
- Make and edit a magazine.
- Learn how to make a book.
- Learn letterpress printing.
- Make candles.
- Make a voodoo doll of your dad. (Revenge will be mine! AHAHAHA)

MAKE MODELS

- Balsa wood gliders
- Metal models
- Ship in a bottle
- Motorcycle models
- Sailboat models
- Car models
- Wood models

- Solid gold models
- Model landscapes

FASHION AND DESIGN

- Make a quilt.
- Weave something on a loom.
- Design a T-shirt.
- Make a dress.
- Make shirts.
- Make curtains. (You can do this fairly easily, but don't use Mom's sheets.)
- Design your own clothes.
- Make a purse.
- Use an old lunch box to create a new one.
- Tie-dye shirts.
- Tie-dye sheets.
- Learn to knit.
- Learn to crochet.
- Learn to do needlework.
- Try painting clothes.
- Make shrink art jewelry.
- Make wood beadwork.
- Make glass beadwork.
- Bedazzle your clothes.
- Make friendship bracelets.
- Make charm bracelets.
- Try nail art.
- Design and make clothes for your pet (or siblings).

Of course, if you really want to get good at making art, or if you just want to learn the basics, you might decide you need to take an art class. In traditional art classes, you might learn how to draw landscapes or people, or how to paint. But did you know there are other kinds of art classes, too? Here are some of the classes you might be able to find near you:

- Art history classes

- Makerspace classes

- Digital art classes

- Digital design classes

- Typography and letterpress classes

- Classes that teach you how to take and/or edit photographs

3

Crafts

BASIC CRAFTS

- Frame a mirror.
- Decorate a frame with paint, or glue-on items.
- Refinish furniture.
- Refinish or decorate old things, like an old watering can.
- Work with nature, making candles, pressing flowers, or using beeswax.
- Paint and hang leaves.
- Decorate rocks.
- Learn how to embroider.

HOLIDAY CRAFTS

- Make a holiday wreath.
- Make a shamrock.
- Learn how to decorate Easter eggs like a professional. (Hint: you can paint them, or glue things on them.)
- Make party hats or party streamers for New Year's Eve.

- For Valentine's Day, make personal cards, make your own chocolate, decorate your own gift box, and make a heart-shaped flower arrangement.
- Pumpkins can be carved, painted, decorated with glue and art supplies, and etched.
- Make holiday ornaments.
- Make a haunted house (for Halloween, not Mother's Day).

GLASS CRAFTS

- Mosaics
- Glass etching
- Stained glass fusing
- Glass mobile making
- Decorating bottles and filling them with custom salad dressing or sauces
- Making glasses or vases from bottles
- Making glass magnets

PAPER CRAFTS

- Make custom boxes.
- Make lampshades.
- Use old playing cards to create art.
- Use wrapping paper to decorate furniture or make frames.
- Use wallpaper to redo furniture.
- Make jewelry, such as paper earrings or hair clips.
- Make paper flowers (they last longer than real flowers).
- Make paper clocks.
- Decorate household items like light switches or an old dresser.

- Make a piñata.
- Make a mobile.
- Make placemats.
- Learn how to make a pop-up card.
- Make a flip book.
- Decorate your bedroom furniture with old wrapping paper.
- Make dishes... well, maybe that's going too far.

FASHION CRAFTS

There are lots of things you can make with a sewing machine in our fashion section, but for those who are slightly less ambitious, there are a lot of things you can make besides clothes.

- Knit socks (not boring ones).
- Make flip flops.
- Make a hat.
- Throw pillows (Don't fill them with rocks like my sister did.)
- Make a scarf.
- Make a finger puppet.
- Make a felt plushie.
- Make a tie.
- Make zucchini covers (fabric covers for the overwhelming number of vegetables you undoubtedly have).

ACTIVITIES

Crafts can get expensive, but they don't have to be. Go to the library and look for craft books, interior design books, or look at old magazines for inspiration. You can also focus on updating old items. For example, use wrapping paper or paint to decorate the garbage can in your room. For supplies, check out rummage sales, thrift stores, and look for free and cheap things on sites like craigslist.org.

Crafts can be the three R's of recycling: Recycle, Reuse, Renew.

4

Be a Basket Case

Every kid since the invention of kids has given their parents a home-made card and a gift certificate that says, "Good for one car wash." I'd bet that Neanderthal children drew pictures on cave walls to tell their parents that they would go kill a wooly mammoth or clean the cave for mom's birthday.

And sure, giving your mom or dad a card promising to do what you're supposed to do anyway is worth a shot. But what if they actually use the gift certificate? I'll tell you what: you end up being forced to do chores you would rather avoid.

This section will provide real ideas for gifts you can create. Obviously, these ideas will work for friends as well as relatives.

ACTIVITIES

- Create a gift basket and fill it with things the recipient will love. For example, I am pretty sure my Old Man would absolutely, positively love a gift basket filled with our favorite foods.

- Create an Emergency gift basket (See chapter 19 "Get ready to survive the apocalypse" for the things you will need.)

- Create a car-trip gift basket.

- Make a date-night gift basket.

- If you are interested in dating, surprise your beau or sweetheart with a gift basket. You wouldn't believe how surprised your significant other will be when you give them a basket full of girly stuff like makeup, soap, deodorant, foot powder, calamine lotion, and hamburger meat.

- If you have a garden and happen to have grown ten thousand zucchinis by accident, using them for a vegetable gift basket is a great idea. (Side note: contact me if you happen to know anyone who needs hundreds of zucchinis.)

- A do-it-yourself dinner or dessert basket is great. Just fill a basket with ingredients. You would be amazed how people react when you give them raw meat for a special occasion!

- If your friends are going on a trip somewhere, you can do themed baskets: a beach basket, a summer-camp basket, or a camping basket.

- Create a game basket, with playing cards, games, and so on.

- Make seasonal baskets for holidays like Halloween or the Fourth of July.

5

Things Not Easy to Put in a Category

When you spend months trying to find activities, you come across a few that are interesting, boring, or just plain goofy. But who are we to judge? Try out one or two of these; you never know if you never try:

- Get a telescope.
- Go bird watching.
- Go hot-air ballooning.
- Wash your dog.
- Get an aquarium.
- Learn magic tricks. (You never know when you will want to cut someone in half.)
- Build a sandcastle (outside, not in the living room).
- Learn how to Hula Hoop.
- Study your genealogy.
- Make a slingshot.
- Learn to play darts.
- Learn about robotics.

- Drive yourself insane with a Rubik's cube.
- Make a scarecrow.
- Learn about Claymation.
- Learn how to fold napkins.
- Get a trampoline or go to one of the places that have trampolines.
- Go to clown school.
- Learn how to be a ventriloquist.
- Make scent bags.
- Make your own garden compost.
- Learn how to tie flies (the ones for fishing, not live flies).
- Start a collection (buttons, rocks, detention slips, cars, stray cats, canes, whatever).
- Learn how to make balloon animals.
- Start bell ringing.
- Learn beekeeping.
- Try herping. (This sounds like a disease, but it's worse; it means searching for amphibians or reptiles.)
- Try cloud watching.
- Learn about yacht racing.
- Try cosplay.
- Learn about falconry.
- Try playing polo.
- Learn about Parkour (otherwise known as the art of injuring one's self by falling).
- Try planking (basically taking naps in uncomfortable places).
- Learn about taxidermy.
- Learn about spelunking (exploring caves).

- Learn about blacksmithing.
- Try gnoming ("borrowing" a garden gnome from a nearby resident and taking it on vacation, sending photographs to the owners of their gnome in various exotic locations—or maybe just at a local restaurant or park if finances are a bit tight).
- Learn to play darts.
- Learn about knife throwing.
- Try ant farming.
- Learn about coffee roasting.
- Try dumpster diving.
- Try gourd crafting.
- Learn how to do henna.
- Practice goat herding.
- Learn ikebana (the Japanese art of flower arranging).
- Write lists. (Trust us; it's a blast.)

6

Overthrow a Country in Seven Easy Steps

**WARNING: INCOMING DAD RANT
CONTROVERSY SCORE XXX
(ENTERTAINMENT LEVEL IS HIGH THOUGH.)**

In school we study history and we learn about wars and political strife throughout history. But we rarely talk about how people rise to power. By reading history and literature, we can see what people do to take over nations. Anyone who has read *Animal Farm* can pretty much sum them up.

1. Promise Utopia. A good place to start is by taking profits and money from corporations and the rich.

2. Divide the people. One group is the victim and the other group the oppressor. In the book *Animal Farm*, the farmers (capitalists) are exploiting the animals (workers).

3. Destroy the education system. Propaganda works best on children, but combined with controlling the messages in the media, the government can indoctrinate the people.

4. Redistribute wealth. A government cannot give anything they do not take from someone else so take the assets from one group and give it to a second.

5. Disarm the population. Hitler, Stalin, Mussolini, Mao Tse Tung, and Castro implemented gun control.

6. Make the population dependent on the government.

Or you could just vote for a Democrat. Just kidding. We know Democrats don't like jokes unless *everybody* thinks they're funny.

ACTIVITIES

* Study history.
* Learn the difference between the two largest American political parties.
* Study economic systems so you know the difference between a conservative, capitalist, socialist, communist, and social democrat.
* Call your representatives and say hi. Or send them an email and you will automatically be added to their email lists and they will tell you when they are visiting near you.

Alternatively: Vote for Alexandra Next Term!!

7

Learn to Cook

There are a lot of things you can cook. In any case, we need to flesh out the book so it doesn't have to be called five things to do without a computer. More importantly, you can have fun learning how to cook and you don't have to cook things you don't want to. Dad only cooks things in the microwave, which is why we have a grudging respect for school lunches.

That said, Dad was kind of surprised that there are recipes for salads. He thought you just tossed a few vegetables in a bowl. It's also kind of cool to learn that you can make food that you usually buy in the store, like bread.

KITCHEN BASICS

- Learn how to follow a recipe.
- Make a vegetarian dinner.
- Learn how to make desserts.
- Learn how to make a no-bake cake.
- Learn how to bake.
- Learn how to make bread.

- Learn how a convection oven works.
- Learn how to make various salads.
- Learn how to make salad dressing.
- Learn how to make soup.
- Learn how to barbeque.
- Learn how to make ice cream.
- Learn how to make frosting.
- Learn how to use a crock pot.
- Learn how to use a wok (aka "a big Oriental frying pan").
- Learn how to make healthy drinks.
- Learn how to dry food for camping.
- Have friends over for a pizza-making party.

BREAKFAST, NOT JUST COLD PIZZA ANYMORE

- French toast
- Bacon and different ways of cooking eggs
- Waffles
- Pancakes
- Potato pancakes
- Crepes

LEARN HOW TO MAKE ETHNIC FOODS

A few of our favorites include:

- Chinese
- Mexican
- Italian
- Indian

- Korean
- Wisconsin (cheese, chips, and beer)

MAIN DISHES

- Barbeque
- Salads
- Fish
- Pasta
- Shrimp
- Crab
- Lobster
- Meat (mystery variety)
- Vegetarian meals
- Pig parts

ODDS AND ENDS

- Make pickles.
- Make coleslaw.
- Prepare radishes (I think they grow on their own).
- Pick a food and make a meal (for example a three-course meal with each dish including something with coconut.)
- Cook game, such as venison (Bambi), duck, goose, and pheasant.
- Make your own trail mix.
- Make Jewish food, such as Tofutti or Malida. (We were not sure if "Jewish" was a type of food, but we found a cookbook called *The 100 Most Jewish Foods* so it must be.)
- Learn how to use a deep fryer.

- Learn how to make jams /preserves.
- Try oil infusion.
- Learn how to can food.
- Prepare dry food for camping.

BREADY FOOD

- Muffins
- Pastries
- Pretzel
- Biscuits
- Coffee cake

GROSS FOOD

- Offal (it may be better if you didn't know)
- Pork belly (bacon)
- Squirrel
- Snails
- Broccoli

DESSERTS

- Make fried ice cream. (It's a real thing.)
- Learn how to make pie crusts.
- Bake a pie. (There are hundreds: blackberry pecan, lingonberry, cherry, blueberry...)
- Bake a cake. (There are also a bazillion different types of cakes.)
- Bake sweet bread such as pumpkin or banana bread.
- Bake cookies such as peanut butter, sugar, or chocolate chip.

- Make ice cream.
- Make sherbet.
- Make fruit drinks.
- Make smoothies.
- Make cupcakes.
- Make caramel corn.
- Make caramel apples or candy apples.
- Make toffee.
- Make chocolate (yes, you can make chocolate).
- Make hard candy.
- Make gum (yes, you can make gum at home).
- Make donuts
- Make veggie desserts (yams with sugar, carrot cake, etc.). Although Alex says that vegetable desserts are sacrilege and therefore should be destroyed...)
- Make crème brûlée. (To make this, you need a blowtorch, which is basically just a baby flamethrower!)

ACTIVITIES

- If cooking and baking were as simple as throwing some ingredients together and baking or frying the food, even Dad could make a decent dinner. Start by learning the basics on how and why food cooks the way it does. For example, why is it harder to fry food with butter compared to oil? How is coconut oil different than corn oil?

- Learning the basics includes understanding how ingredients work together. If you have ever watched one of those cooking shows, it is inevitable that the hosts whisper something like,

"Contestant number two forgot to add baking powder and now his cupcake is going to blow up like a hydrogen bomb." (Technically it would collapse like a black hole.) Find a very basic cookbook which explains the fundamentals of cooking.

- Find a fun and easy recipe—not as easy as Dad's peanut butter cookie recipe. (One cup peanut butter, one cup sugar, one egg, mix, and cook in oven at 450 degrees until done.)

- Pick a type of food you would like to learn how to make, such as bread. Experiment with a variety of recipes for that type of food.

- Pick a theme and try to make a dinner around that theme, such as a southern barbeque or Chicago ribs.

- Be social and ask your family or friends to cook with you.

8

Have a Theme Party

If you ever need an excuse to throw a party, why not have a theme party?

THEMES

- Hawaiian luau
- Scavenger hunt
- Casino night
- Karaoke party
- Spa party
- Movie or TV party (technically this is screen time but at least you're not sitting around by yourself.)
- Movie themed party (Disney favorites, Zombies, Romantic Comedy)
- Pre or Post-Prom party
- Outdoor movie party
- Easter egg hunt (You can hide more than eggs or candy!)
- Volunteer party (Find a cause and bring your friends along.)
- Paintball party

- Slip-N-Slide (also known as Break-A-Bone) party
- Murder mystery board game party
- Tea party
- Game night party
- Card party (where you make holiday cards, killing two birds with one stone)

9

Talk to Yourself (Not just a Sign of Insanity Anymore!)

My super studious sister is applying to private school and filling out dozens of applications. Each application is different, but most ask students to describe themselves and discuss what motivates them. The questions do actually help students to identify what they like and ultimately to determine what they can do to create a meaningful and joyful life. So what the heck? Pretend you are applying to college and ask your friends or yourself questions.

- What do you value most?
- Do you believe that there is value in failing?
- What do you do to relax?
- What activities are important to you?
- What is a hidden talent you have?
- Do you have any role models?
- What do you want to do when you grow up?
- Describe an interest.

- What inspires you?
- Who is your favorite superhero?
- If you left your house in an emergency, what would you take?
- What would you like people to know about you that they do not?
- How is a teenager's brain different from an adult's?

10

Write Your Obituary

Dad says we should respect old people. He also says respect is earned, not automatic. To confuse matters, he also claims every politician over the age of twelve is an idiot. With that in mind, we picked up a book called, *30 Lessons for Living: Tried and True Advice from the Wisest Americans.* Okay, they were not as wise as Albert Einstein, and were basically just old people, but the old people did have some good points, some of which we have already mentioned. They also included:

- Treat your body like you will need it for a hundred years.
- Happiness is a choice, not a condition.
- Say yes to opportunity.
- Travel more.
- Chose a career with intrinsic value rather than for financial reward.
- Make the most out of any job.
- One of the most interesting ideas presented in the book had to do with vices and dying. Many people don't care about their health or vices and think that the worst thing that can happen from smoking or being obese is that they die a few years earlier.

It turns out that having an illness that destroys the quality of your life because you smoke and have a hole in your throat to talk through and which prevents you from doing the sports you love will diminish the quality of your life.

ACTIVITIES

Why not take some time and write your obituary? Okay, if that is too morbid for you, do one or more of the following activities.

- Why not create a vision of what you want to accomplish in your life?
- How about creating a one-year, five-year, and ten-year plan?
- Create a bucket list of things to do, places to go, such as traveling, writing a song, going to college.

11

Volunteer

There are thousands of volunteering opportunities. If you decide to volunteer, not only are you helping others, but you will benefit as well. There is something inherently rewarding in helping others. But more than that, it gets you out of the house, gives you the chance to meet new people, and you may discover new skills and interests. In addition, volunteering lets you combine things you like doing with helping others. A few ways to volunteer include:

- Volunteer at an animal shelter.
- Help with a food drive.
- Volunteer at a food bank.
- Volunteer to help seniors.
- Help out at your local library.
- Become a docent (people who help you in galleries, museums, and grocery stores).
- Tutor kids in subjects you are good at (or just tutor much younger kids).
- Raise money for a good cause.
- Build a house (seriously, check out Habitat for Humanity).
- Join the Red Cross.

There are some well-established organizations that may need help such as:

- American Cancer Society
- Big Brothers Big Sisters
- Guide Dogs for the Blind
- Make-a-Wish Foundation
- Conservation Organizations
- Community Theater Companies
- Youth Centers such as the YMCA

There are also some organizations that allow you to live away from home for part of the summer, such as the Student Conservation Association. You could also find out how to start your own organization and maybe plant trees, clean up a neighborhood, or help remove graffiti.

12

Become Politically Active

You don't have to be old enough to vote to be politically active. In fact, being young can be an advantage. Young people protesting makes good news stories that are hard to ignore.

ACTIVITIES

- Rally for a cause.
- Write letters to a newspaper's editorial department. (Newspapers are like really big thin books with more/less pictures, depending on what you read.)
- Write letters to politicians about things that are important to you.
- Attend meetings where decisions are made (city budget meeting, Parent-Teacher Association meetings, school board meeting etc.).
- Obtain support from adults, such as your school principal.
- Create petitions.
- Join groups that are politically active.
- Become an advocate for a cause such as saving endangered species.
- Work on a campaign.
- Run for office. (Vote for Alexandra next term!)

13

Learn How to Save a Life

Some of this book may seem glib, but the sad truth is that kids kill themselves. Of course, teens are sometimes moody and dramatic, but depression and suicide are also very real things that deserve more recognition.

SUICIDE PREVENTION

There are specific warnings which include:

- Talking about wanting to die or to kill themselves.
- Looking for a way to kill themselves, like searching online or buying a gun.
- Talking about feeling hopeless or having no reason to live.
- Talking about feeling trapped or in unbearable pain.
- Talking about being a burden to others.
- Increasing the use of alcohol or drugs.
- Acting anxious or agitated or behaving recklessly.
- Sleeping too little or too much.
- Withdrawing or isolating themselves.

- Showing rage or talking about seeking revenge.
- Experiencing extreme mood swings.

There are also five steps to help someone who may be suicidal. They are:

- Ask.
- Keep them safe.
- Be there.
- Help them connect.
- Follow up.

If a friend or family member needs help, the National Suicide Prevention number is:

1-800-273-8255.

OTHER LIFESAVING SKILLS

- Learn self-defense and you may save your own life.
- Learn CPR.
- Learn the basics of first aid.
- Learn wilderness first aid.
- Train to be a lifeguard.

CHAPTER

14

Learn What to Do When You Need Help

We can't really fix other people's problems, but we are often not expected to either. Sometimes you just need to show up and be present.

According to my dad, most problems are not unique. They may be painful, but they are not unique. There are people who can help, people who have experience with specific issues. We considered adding a list of resources for kids who need help with real life problems.

Unfortunately, the number of serious problems you or your friends may encounter is endless. The reality is that many people may have a terrible home life. Parents may be getting a divorce; they may be physically or emotionally abusive, addicted to drugs or alcohol, unable to provide a basic level of care, have serious financial problems, or they may be homeless. Your friends may have the same problems as their parents, or they may be engaging in dangerous and stupid activities. To add to these issues, people suffer from an endless list of mental health issues, such as depression, schizophrenia, anxiety disorders, and·borderline personality disorder, to name a few. There are also specific situations that can cause problems, such as deaths, illnesses and injuries, parents abandoning their children, or going to jail.

All problems have one thing in common. There are adults willing to help you.

Any idiot can post stupid things on the internet, such as the benefits of using heroin. This is worth repeating: If you have a problem or suspect that a friend has a problem, talk to an adult. You can always start with a doctor, a school counselor, a teacher, or you can call a helpline. Most cities and counties have government workers or referral services.

CHAPTER

15

Learn a Language and about Different Cultures

Take some time to learn a language, or about a different culture.

SUCH AS

- Spanish
- Chinese
- Japanese
- English (oh, wait…)
- Pig Latin
- Klingon
- American Sign Language (ASL)
- British Sign language (BSL)

Learning a language in school is great, but what if you want to learn a language that's not taught in your school? There are literally a ton of free online programs. In fact, a quick google search came up with a website that provides over 50 language learning sites, plus there are countless tutor sites to help you if you are already taking a class. In addition, you can buy software such as Babble. Most libraries also have CDs with basic language learning programs.

But why not do more than just learn about a language? Why not learn about the culture too? Here are a few things you can do:

- Plan a trip to a foreign country.
- Find people who speak the language you want to learn and have them tutor you. For example, find a senior center and see if any retirees would help you, or find a classmate whose native language is not English.
- Read books and travel guides.
- Find current news stories about a different country.
- Interview people who have lived in a country that interests you.

CHAPTER
16

Daydream

"How about structured daydreaming?"

Obviously Dad is not clear on the concept of daydreaming.

KEEP A DIARY

We promise it's not the same as the journal one. Well… for the most part anyway.

When I think of keeping a diary, I think of a book my sister could find and use to extort pretty much anything from me. But according to Richard Wiseman (an author), expressing gratitude, thinking about a perfect future, and affectionate writing have been scientifically proven to work at making people happier. In other words, it's an extortion device that's supposed to make you happy (until your sister finds it). But hey, it came from a Wiseman. Quite literally.

Wiseman's diary outline is summarized as follows:

- Monday—write three things you are thankful for.
- Tuesday—write about terrific times in your life.
- Wednesday—write about your future.

- Thursday—write a letter to someone important to you.
- Friday—reflect on the week and write down three things that went well for you.
- Saturday and Sunday—forget you even have a dairy until Monday comes again. (That one's from us).

CHAPTER

17

Sports

Baseball is 90% mental and the other half is physical. —Yogi Berra

Sure, there are some kids who appear to be naturally athletic, and it helps if you are six feet five and can run a 90-second mile. But there are plenty of sports that are fun and do not require a perfect body. There are also individual sports (like biking and skiing) where you can be terrible but who cares because you're not competing with anyone. This list is intentionally random. We hope you find a sport that you have not considered before.

- Badminton
- Boxing
- Kickboxing
- Cycling BMX
- Cycling mountain biking
- Riding a unicycle
- Cycling street
- Football
- Jump roping

- Fencing (YAY SWORDS!)
- Golf
- Gymnastics
- Handball
- Floor hockey
- Judo
- Rowing
- Rugby
- Sailing

- Windsurfing
- Parasailing
- Zip lining
- Swimming
- Diving
- Synchronized swimming
- Table Tennis
- Tennis
- Taekwondo
- Karate
- Triathlon training
- Volleyball
- Water volleyball
- Polo
- Water polo
- Wrestling
- Weightlifting
- Pole Vaulting
- Tumbling
- Alpine skiing
- Tobogganing
- Boomeranging
- Curling
- Ice skating
- Rollerblading
- Roller skating
- Riding a scooter
- Skateboarding
- Snowshoe hiking
- Cross country skiing
- Figure skating
- Ice hockey
- Hockey indoor
- Speed skating
- Archery
- Baseball
- Softball
- Canoeing
- Kayaking
- Inflatable Kayaking
- Whitewater rafting
- Tubing
- Cricket
- Croquet
- Handball
- Lacrosse
- Rugby
- Sailing
- Shooting
- Windsurfing
- Water motor sports
- Jet skiing
- Waterskiing
- Beach volleyball
- Frisbee
- Golf Frisbee

- Flag football
- Floor hockey
- Surfing
- Darts
- Horseback riding
  (not sure if this is a sport
  for you or the horse)
  Water balloons
  (do this inside and Mom
  will give you a work-out)
- Paintball
- Miniature golf
- Trampoline
  (not recommended
  unless you want to be on
  American home videos of
  people hurting themselves)
- Scuba diving
- Bowling
- Bocce ball
- Fly fishing
- Fishing
- Deep Sea Fishing
- Outdoor rock climbing
  (an alternative to indoor
  rock climbing)
- Indoor rock climbing
  (an alternative to outdoor
  rock climbing)
- Skydiving (falling from a
  plane may not be a sport
  but it makes you sweat so
  we included it here.)
- Hang Gliding
- Snorkeling
- Aerobics
- Cross training
- Bird watching
  (Not a sport but we need
  hundreds of things to do so
  go look for a bird.)
- Hunting (It is like watching
  birds but doing it in order
  to kill them. May not be
  a sport from the animals'
  point of view.)
- Pickleball (No, it's not
  played with vegetables.)
- Tetherball (also known as
  that ball that gives you a
  bloody nose)
- Yoga (Yoga is not a sport
  you say? Well, I did it once
  and could not move for a
  week, so it's a sport.)
- Juggling (Sure, it's a sport.)
- Tumbling

18

Get Ready to Survive the Apocalypse

"Alex, I'm getting ready for the apocalypse."

"Calvin, relax. It's only a math test. I can help you study."

"No, I mean like Armageddon."

"Oh God. What did you upset Mom about this time?"

Since we live in California, there are constant warnings about being prepared for an emergency. But no matter where you live, you should prepare for an emergency. This is what we have figured out you need to do to survive the apocalypse.

- Don't die (pro tip).
- Hoard (like a rat).
- Get a lot of clean water; a well is even better. (Well = infinite water.)
- Gather non-perishable food. If things really go bad, the electricity will be nonexistent.

- Optional, but recommended: Move to a moderate climate, so you don't freeze to death or burn to a crisp. (Wouldn't want that water supply to freeze or evaporate.)
- Stay indoors (like a really long staycation).
- As soon as society begins to unravel, raid your local supermarkets.
- Get a recording of a shotgun to scare looters (or the real thing works too).
- "Borrow" all that "extra" propane (gas) from your local hardware store. (Use bolt cutters, which they conveniently sell.)
- Get LOTS of potatoes. People have lived off potatoes for hundreds of years in Ireland/England or someplace. Also saw this "documentary" about a guy stranded on Mars and only ate potatoes grown in poop.
- Don't let your neighbors know you have a stockpile of food and water.
- Don't expect the government to save you.
- Hunker down with your supplies and wait.

Waiting…

Still Waiting…

Done!

Congratulations! You survived the apocalypse! Now have fun in the post-apocalyptic world!

(Dad says to take this seriously and told me ALL the stuff I missed because he's crazy when it comes to provisions and stuff, so here we go…)

- Make a plan for your family in an emergency.
- Find a way to cook your food (like a propane stove).
- Get a first aid kit for minor injuries.
- Get a chainsaw for BIG injuries (just kidding) but a few tools are handy, like a crowbar if you live in earthquake country.
- Put an emergency kit in each car and keep one at home.
- If your family has no emergency kit, make one and give it to your parents as a gift.
- Get pet food if you have a pet (or younger sibling - Ow! Older sibling works too.)
- Plan for a 24-hour, three-day, seven-day, one-month, and three-month-to-a-year emergency.

19

Write

- Writing is fun, but you don't need to write an essay like you do in school; it can be anything!
- Write a book on a hundred (or more) things for teens to do and send it to us so we can make more money.
- Write a story. (It's good exercise for your creative bits.)
- Write a poem.
- Write a screenplay.
- Write a TV show.
- Write a novel.
- Write a musical.
- Write a comedy.
- Write a fan letter.
- Write to a politician.
- Write a letter to your future self.
- Write letters to relatives. (Everyone loves mail.)
- Type a book.
- Type a story.
- Type a poem.

- Create your own cards.
- Create postcards.
- Write a comic.
- Create a poster.
- Use a typewriter.

Keep in mind, you're welcome to send us suggestions for activities.

20

Singing, Dancing, and Making Noise

"I think an animal is dying in the shower!"

"What?" Sure enough, we can hear the faint sound of what appears to be some sort of wild beast crying in pain.

"Oh wait, that's just Dad singing."

TRADITIONAL SINGING

- Choir
- Rap
- Rock and Roll
- Jazz
- Humming (not really singing but close)
- Shower (probably even less like singing)

DANCE STYLES

- Rock and Roll
- Tango

- Balboa (Balboa is a type of swing dancing.)
- Belly dance
- Breakdance
- Lindy hop
- Ballroom
- Hip Hop
- Hootchy-kootchy
- Hokey pokey
- Hustle (It's a dance, not what you do before school.)
- Jiving
- Pogo (So you just jump up and down, but hey it's a dance…)
- Polka (Old people love it.)
- Texas swing
- Rain dance
- Robot dance
- Rumba
- Salsa
- Samba
- Scottish country dancing
- Shag (Not the fuzzy rug but a type of swing.)
- Shim sham
- Shimmy
- Zouk-Lambada (Not sure what it is but you get to say: "Hey Mom, I am going to Zouk tonight.")
- Zumba
- Zydeco dancing

PLAY AN INSTRUMENT

After I bought a drum set from Deaf Eddy for twenty dollars, Dad decided I could play any instrument that did not include sticks.

Here are a few instruments. These are atypical but have the advantage of driving your parents crazy. (A few of them are drums but don't tell Dad.)

- Electric banjo
- Electric harp
- Ukulele
- Mandolin
- Accordion
- Electric Accordion (just kidding)
- Bagpipes
- Bassoon
- Dung-dkar (It's a shell trumpet.)
- Firebird guitar
- Flumpet
- Harmonica
- Heckelphone (I have no idea what it is, but it sounds fun.)
- Kaval
- Nose Flute (Not sure if it's played with the nose.)
- Ophicleide
- Pasiyak
- Whistle
- Pipe organ (Ask Mom before you set one of those up in the garage.)
- Piano
- Pocket trumpet
- Reed organ
- Sackbut
- Sarrusophone (Might need to go to France to get one.)
- Saxhorn
- Serpent (The instrument, not the creature.)
- Shakuhachi (My dad thinks this is a type of sushi.)
- Siren whistle
- Saw blade (Technically a tool but some drums are just buckets.)
- Tarogato

- Tible
- Trombone
- Tuba
- Tube trumpet
- TipongTxistu (Learn this word and you will be a master at the game of Scrabble.)
- Vuvuzela (Also helpful when playing Scrabble.)
- Cello
- Chapman stick
- Cittern
- Clavichord
- Diddley bow
- Double bass
- Guitar synthesizer
- Steel guitar
- Double neck guitar
- Triple neck guitar
- Lute
- Lyre
- Mandolin
- Doorbell (Not technically an instrument.)
- Oud
- Washtub bass
- Conga drum
- Drum set
- Melodeon
- Saxophone
- Oboe

ACTIVITIES

- Unless you're some musical prodigy you will probably need lessons and an instrument. Many music stores will let you rent an instrument.

- Ask your music teacher if they know anyone who can tutor you.

- Ask your music teacher if they have any extra instruments. (Lots of kids donate instruments when they decide to switch instruments or stop playing.)

- Go online and see if you can find private lessons.

- Ask a friend if they want to learn an instrument with you. Group lessons can be fun and less expensive than private classes.

- If you are not musically inclined but like music, find a band that needs help. You can learn to mix music, help record music, write songs, or create videos.

- If you already know how to play, start a band.

21

Give Your Parents a Coronary

(Written by Dad)

Not technically a Dad rant but we're labeling it anyway:

INCOMING DAD RANT— CONTROVERSY SCORE X

If you want to give your parents a heart attack, I recommend doing one or more of the following.

- Try to shock your dad by saying "I have some free time this weekend. Are there any projects you need help with or extra chores I can do?"
- Vacuum (the house not the lawn).
- Make your own hair, dentist, and doctor appointments.
- Clean your room.
- Fold your clothes.
- Pick up after yourself.

- Don't leave your stuff in the middle of the floor _____.
- Make sure your room does not smell like a teenager lives there.
- Clean parts of the house that are behind small doors (under the sink, the refrigerator, bathroom cabinets.)
- Clean out the family car.
- Give the dog a bath.
- Ask your mom what a comb is. (Hint: it looks like a fork.)
- Do your homework.
- Smile! (Especially if your mom spent piles of cash on braces.)
- Give her a hug.
- Say the T word (Thank You).
- Trim your nails but don't leave your nails clippings on the table.
- Remember there is no such thing as a dirty laundry fairy.
- Wake up when your alarm blasts.
- Remember doors can open and close.
- Yard work is not optional.
- Shovel the driveway. If there is no snow, sweep the driveway and garage.
- Make Mom a card just for the heck of it.
- Clean the windows on the outside.
- Wash out the garbage cans. (Yes, they do need to be hosed out once in a while.)
- Clean the gutters.
- Clean the basement or garage.
- Water the plants.

ALTERNATIVELY (NOT WRITTEN BY DAD.)

Now, if you *really* want to give them a heart attack, I recommend something a bit more along the lines of, "Guess what, Dad? You're going to be a grandfather sooner that you thought!" Extra points if you get him when he's drinking coffee.

22

How to Make Your Parents Appreciate You

EXCELLENT IDEAS

- Be as annoying as possible so they appreciate how not annoying you are normally.
- Show them you know table manners by not using them for a day.
- Show them how many chores you do, by not doing any of them for a day.
- Show them how your room is usually clean, by not cleaning it for a while.
- Show how well you play the trombone by waking them up at four AM with a tune.
- Show how neat you are normally by piling all your stuff in the middle of the living room.
- Show how artistic you are by drawing on the walls with a sharpie.

- Show how strong you are by ripping a phonebook in half. (Note: use the phonebook from Buford Wyoming, City Population: 1)
- Show how clean you are by not bathing for a day (or two).
- Show them how agreeable you are normally by complaining nonstop for a day.
- Show them how intelligent you are by making counterfeit money.
- Show them how much you love them by not using the ideas on this list.

WARNING: INCOMING DAD RANT
CONTROVERSY SCORE XX

(My dad is in one of his moods. He's clearly talking to himself.)

"What is wrong with you kids? Do you think parents go to work on Monday and say this? 'Hey Bob, how are you? I had a great weekend forcing my kids to clean their rooms, yelling at my daughter to stop leaving dirty dishes under her pillow, and then I spent half an hour trying to find our pet in the four-foot high weeds because my son forgot to cut the grass.' No, parents don't want to yell at their kids and despite what you think, telling kids to do their chores is not an older person hobby."

So if you are like I am and your parents have given you hundreds if not thousands of chores, plus the hundreds of homework assignments given out every day, and you don't want to drive your parents nuts, get organized and stay on top of your chores, school, and other activities.

- Get a filing cabinet and make a folder for important papers.
- Get a checkbook and track your spending.

- Get an app or pocket planner to keep track of your schedule.

- Use your phone calendar to record all tasks and to set reminders.

- Declutter. It's hard to find stuff if your desk, room, backpack, and locker are all disorganized and filled with old papers.

- Use wall calendars.

For some reason it seems that people who are naturally organized want to help us disorganized challenged people with elaborate, color-coded, three-ring binders that go into color-coded boxes, that are put in color-coded filing cabinets. You get the idea. The trick is to figure out a way to organize your homework, chores, personal hygiene, and activities in a way that you can manage.

23

Earn Money

ERRAND AND GIG JOBS

- Be a parent helper.
- Babysit.
- Do lawn maintenance.
- Be a personal assistant.
- Be a personal organizer.
- Be a computer assistant.
- Be a web page designer.
- Be a dog walker.
- Be a Sign Spinner. (You know the people with signs standing on the side of the road. Best if you don't have to wear a costume like a dog spinning a sign for a dog wash.)
- Be a referee through the parks and recs department.
- House sit, or dog sit.
- Sell pre-made dinners. Lots of busy families would love to have simple-to-make dinners.
- Sell baked goods.

OUTDOOR JOBS

- Landscaping
- Delivery services (Not really outdoor, but not stuck in a mall either.)
- Construction work
- Camp counselor
- Agricultural jobs such as picking apples
- Lifeguard
- Work for the parks department.
- Get in an accident and sue (not recommended).

SEASONAL JOBS

- Fair workers
- Amusement park worker
- Public jobs (zoo, library, tour guides)
- Government jobs. Many municipalities hire teens for all sorts of summer jobs.
- Hotel workers
- Tourist traps. Oops, I meant the tourism industry.

FIRST TIME JOBS

- Try the obvious places, like restaurants and retail stores.
- Event workers, including jobs with caterers, at stadiums, weddings, etc.
- Call center worker
- Movie theater jobs
- Gas stations

- Receptionist
- Temporary jobs (There are temporary agencies that find temporary workers for employers.)
- Campaign jobs

JOBS AWAY FROM HOME

- Camp counselor
- Teaching English abroad
- Resort jobs
- Agricultural jobs

AVOID SCAMS

Most jobs that say you can work from home or earn money by surfing the web are scams. Most but not all work-at-home jobs are a scam. Also, these jobs involve staring at a screen.

Avoid jobs that do not pay in money. These include survey taking, testing mobile apps, jobs that give you points which you can redeem for things.

Avoid jobs that don't pay at all, such as the organization that lets you work on a farm for free food and a place to stay.

START A BUSINESS OR FREELANCE

"Hey Dad, I figured out a great job. I am going to sell products online."

"Great! What are you going to sell?"

"You know, stuff we don't need, like your golf clubs, skis, eyeglasses, and your car."

Selling stuff online is not always a lucrative business if you are simply selling things you own. Then again, why not try to sell the junk that is cluttering up your room and garage?

GET RICH QUICK

The absolutely best way to get rich quick is to sell this book. With a minimum order of 10 books, we will sell them to you for 25% off the suggested retail price.

Just go to our website: www.mindfulcynic.com and click on the get-rich-quick button.

24

Take a Test Even Dad Can Pass

Take a personality test. Probably the most popular is the Myer-Briggs test. But there are others such as personality colors. To be fair, most personality tests are junk science. That said, the goal is not to cast yourself in some mold based on a few questions but rather glean insight into yourself. Sure, there are plenty of them online, but sometimes it's nice to take out the pen and paper and do it the old-fashioned way. Oh no, it happened! I sound like Dad! Nooooooooo! I didn't want to get old this young! Noooooo! Also, true personality tests are scientific resources, and therefore not found on someone's Weebly page, just saying.

CHAPTER

25

Games

THESE ARE A FEW FUN GAMES I FOUND

- Wits and Wagers
- Pokémon (The card version, as we are restricted to non-technological devices.)
- Chess
- Risk
- Magic: The Gathering
- Jenga
- Connect Four
- Monopoly
- Life
- Blackjack
- Poker
- Cribbage
- Sheepshead
- Bridge
- Apples to Apples

- Scrabble
- Upwords (which is like Scrabble five tiles high)
- Quirkle
- Settlers of Catan
- Backgammon
- Dungeons and Dragons (It's been around long enough, and we seriously recommend it.)
- Card games, such as Exploding Kittens and Unstable Unicorns
- Make Up Game.

Obviously, these are only a few of the games you can get. There are entire stores devoted to games. Heck, you can even make up a game. My friends and I use Google docs to play tag. The person who is tagged has to pick a thing to do for a day, such as talking with a hand puppet, talking in third person all day, or ending every sentence with "your momma."

INCOMING DAD RANT— CONTROVERSY SCORE XXX

When I was your age, we had a rock and a knife and a board to scratch out a tic-tac-toe game. Now there are millions of games. Heck, there are dozens of variations of the same game: Monopoly, Empire Monopoly, Game of Thrones Monopoly, and Socialist Monopoly, to name a few. With so many games, there must be a game that you and your friends would like. The game stores are generally organized by the type of game such as:

- Two player games (Chess, Checkers, and that sort of thing).
- Multiplayer elimination games, where, as the name would imply, people are eliminated.

- Multiplayer non-elimination games.
- Role-playing games.
- Economic and strategy games.
- Games for the entire family.
- Games that require physical skills.

Talking and joking games such as Cards Against Humanity, which is really fun (and oops!) very inappropriate for kids, so don't play it with your parents.

You can even find stores that have a game night, so you don't even have to buy the games. Some stores have open game nights where they try new games; others have regular meetings with the same game.

One last thing. Sure, you can play video games online with your friends, but it's not the same as actually getting together in the same room to play a game. And if you order a pizza, you may actually take a break from playing the game and talk to each other.

26

Live for Less

Tickets to a New York Broadway show can be pricy, especially if you live in Kansas and have to add in the cost of a bus or plane ticket. Tickets to the Super Bowl can cost $4,000 or more and you may not like either team. If you want to see a NASCAR race, it can cost over 20 million dollars (assuming you want to see it from the drivers' seat). Music is no different. Justin Bieber tickets can cost over a thousand dollars, and your parents could spend additional untold millions on a therapist to try to figure out why you would spend that kind of money to see Justin Bieber.

Obviously, some sports like hunting are not great spectator sports, but most high schools and colleges have dozens of teams so you should be able to find one you like.

Live performances, sporting events, and concerts can be insanely expensive, but they don't have to be; and while not as dramatic as some sporting events, there are countless lectures and book signings. Often these are advertised in weekly papers or the Sunday edition of your local paper.

SUGGESTIONS

1. Attend high school or college games.

2. Attend high school or college concerts and plays,

3. Some venues offer discount tickets for weekday performances or matinees.

4. Some venues offer discount tickets the day of the show.

5. Look for lecture series.

6. Find sports with fewer fans (water polo or lacrosse).

7. If you don't have any money, simply ask the attendant if you can watch for free. While this won't work for professional games or events, it seems unlikely that you will be turned away from a high school play for lack of funds.

27

New Age

If you don't know what New Age beliefs are, that's something you should learn about from someone who is not still in middle/high school. To those of you who do know what it is, many people believe that a lot of New Age stuff seems like dog poo with whipped cream on top. That said, exploring New Age beliefs can be fun and help provide insight into your own personality. For example, Tarot cards include cards about success, failure, death, courage, and creativity. Using Tarot cards as a tool to contemplate bigger issues can be both fun and insightful. Likewise, astrology may seem like baloney, but thinking about your personality characteristics is a great idea.

- Learn about your astrological sign.
- Learn how to do astrology readings for your friends.
- Read about the studies with psychics. For example, the military successfully used psychics for remote viewing.
- Read about how psychics have been tested.
- Read about "normal" people who had psychic experiences (Abraham Lincoln, Mark Twain, and General Patton).
- Use Tarot cards as a source of inspiration and meditation.
- Read about people who have had a near-death experience.

- Study complementary and integrated healthcare.

- Study how our consciousness affects the material world.

- Learn about the chakras.

- Learn about natural cures.

- Some natural cures, such as Prevagen, which is derived from jellyfish, have been shown to be complete nonsense, while others such as kava (a root stem) can cause liver damage. However, acupuncture does have medical benefits. Likewise, chiropractic, cupping, meditation, yoga, Tai Chi, and Qigong all have proven health benefits.

- Read books by spiritual teachers such Wayne W. Dyer or the Dalai Lama.

- Lean how to meditate.

- Develop your own spiritual practice. (See *Self-help for Dummies.*)

MORE ON TAROT CARDS (BY DAD)

If you think Tarot cards are a deck of cards used by frauds to predict the future, you are right. If you think they are a deck of cards that allows for creative self-expression and personal discovery and growth, you are also right.

Our family uses the Voyager deck, but there are all sorts of decks. Tarot cards fall into two broad categories, the Major Arcana and the Minor Arcana.

The Major Arcana cards represent archetypal characteristics, which means typical characteristics. Most of us have aspects of the archetypal characteristics (leader, healer, warrior, etc.). Pulling a Major card such as the fool allows us to focus on the areas in our life where, for better or worse, we rely on faith.

The Minor Archana reflect situations we encounter daily. They are the numbered cards and are divided into sets. The "Ones' focus on our intellect (thoughts, reason, logic); the "Twos" focus on emotions (jealousy, love, hate).

In her book, *The Creative Tarot: A Modern Guide to an Inspired Life* by Jessa Crispin, the author includes a description of each card which can be used for self-reflection. She also offers suggestions for using the cards for creativity. For example, she pulls three cards, and the first represents the head, the second the heart, and the third the body. The same three-card drawing can be used to identify what is blocking your creativity.

She also offers suggestions for a seven-card reading. The first card is you, the second is the project, the third and fourth are your obstacles, the fifth is your tool to overcome the obstacles, the sixth is your next step, and the seventh is the outcome. Try giving your friends a Tarot reading. It could be a fun activity! You will need a deck of Tarot cards and a book to help interpret the cards.

28

Treat Yourself like a Cat

I was reading the label on my cat's catnip and it said cats need ten things. I thought this applies to people as well.

1. Independence
2. Exercise
3. Scratching
4. Stimulation
5. Privacy
6. Exploration
7. Hunting
8. Care
9. Interaction
10. Comfort

So maybe we don't need to hunt, but if you have a pet you should take care of it, and that involves much more than feeding it. Likewise, we should think about our own needs and wants and how we are getting them fulfilled.

TWO

THINGS THEY DON'T TEACH YOU IN SCHOOL BUT SHOULD

CHAPTER

29

Self-Help for Dummies

Any library or bookstore has a section called "self-help," which is ironic since you are looking for an author to tell you how to help yourself. In fact, there are so many self-help books on basic topics that we will skip self-help books on topics such as Dieting, or How to Get Rich Selling Your Organs. Instead we will suggest a few books that may help change your attitudes, add a spiritual component to your life, or help you to try and live a conscious life.

- *The Art of Happiness: A Handbook for Living*—The Dalai Lama and Howard C. Cutler
- *Real Magic: Creating Miracles in Everyday Life*—Wayne Dyer
- *Man's Search for Meaning*—Viktor Frankl
- *Men are from Mars, Women are from Venus*—John Grey
- *Awaken the Giant Within*—Anthony Robbins
- *The Power of Positive Thinking*—Norman Vincent Peale

30

Have a Talk with Your Parent or Guardian

INCOMING DAD RANT— CONTROVERSY SCORE XX

If you are a teenager, there are six things you need to do (according to Dad anyway.)

1. Do well in school.

2. Take care of your chores.

3. Take care of your body.

4. Practice being a loving and compassionate person.

5. Don't do stupid things.

6. Be forward thinking.

Nobody can expect perfection. So yeah, you may forget to shave or put on your acne medicine; you may forget to do your laundry or bomb a test; and you may act your age and do dumb things and want immediate gratification. It's all part of growing up, or something like that.

ACTIVITIES

Most parents want to know that their kids are reasonable. If you want more freedom, try some of the following:

- Have a conversation with your parents and reiterate that you are for the most part doing what you should be doing (as above). As a result, you should get more control over your life.

- On the other hand, if you are not doing these things, get started.

- Demonstrate that you are forward thinking. Forward thinking is more than just deciding what to do after high school. It includes creating good life-long habits, such as getting exercise on a regular basis and avoiding becoming addicted to crack cocaine or following the Kardashians.

CHAPTER

31

Understand the Teenage Brain

(By Dad with help from the siblings)

INCOMING DAD RANT— (SOMEWHAT INTERESTING)

I am not a neuroscientist, so I looked this up on the computer. The teenage brain has three main parts with fancy names, but I call them the crocodile brain, the emotional part, and the thinking or gray part (called the prefrontal cortex). The crocodile brain is essentially the primitive part of your brain that says, "Ahh! We've been poisoned! Throw up!" Pretty useful unless you are motion sick in the car and your brain thinks you have been poisoned.

The emotional part of your brain develops before the thinking part. As a little kid, you show your emotions to get what you want. Want an ice cream? Stomp your feet, scream, and make a scene.

The thinking part of your brain is developing and will continue to do so until your mid 20's. In your teenage years, its "default" can seem to be the five-year-old brain. When your parents tell you to do something you don't want to do, your brain may default to a temper tantrum with the result being a snarky comment such as rolling your eyes and saying, "Yeah, right!" It's perfectly natural because you have much more experience with the emotional part of your brain. If you catch yourself reacting like a five-year old, just apologize and move on.

Do you know what else your teenage brain likes to use your emotional brain for? Risk judgement. So next time you succumb to peer pressure or can't seem to realize there are consequences for your actions until you do them, you now know who to blame. Thanks brain!

Your brain is also shedding the parts that are no longer needed. The technical name for this is "pruning" which is kind of funny since most technical words are much more impressive. The adage, "use it or lose it," really does apply to the teenage brain. Does that mean that after not riding my bike for three years I will forget how to do it? No, because you use the skills of balancing, walking, and coordinating your legs and arms every day. But if you were fluent in French in Kindergarten and have not spoken since then, your brain has probably cut that link to make room for some new information. (This could also explain why your parents can't help you with your math). A weird bit of trivia is that to aid in the pruning it appears that your brain cells shrink when you are asleep.

The implications of the changes in teenage brain growth means that as a teenager you should exercise your mind. Instead of being apathetic and losing skills, it's time to strengthen them.

The other implication is, don't do drugs. Your brain is already undergoing a constant growth and reorganization, even while you sleep. Adding crack cocaine, marijuana, and alcohol is a very bad idea, as it will disturb the process. People claim marijuana is harmless, but I seriously doubt that. It would be unethical, to say the least, to give pot to kids to see if it causes brain damage. Also, there is evidence (other than your stoner uncle) that kids who smoke pot have permanent brain damage. The brain damage appears to make you slower rather than dumber. (If you don't know the difference, use your brain to think about it.) Avoid drugs and let your brain grow. As the comedian Ron White says, "You can't fix stupid."

ACTIVITIES

- Get a book on teenage development.

- Show this chapter to your parents with a generic, "I am sorry if I gave you a knee-jerk response."

- Avoid damaging your brain. Drugs are bad, but they are particularly bad for kids with growing brains. You would not give an infant marijuana so why would you give it to yourself?

- Learn to apologize. You may accidentally slip up and act like a five-year-old, but that doesn't mean you can't say you're sorry and move on.

- Watch your behavior and notice when you are not acting your age.

32

A List is Worth 1,000 Words

Unless you have a magic genie hidden away, if you want to accomplish most things, you will need to have a goal and a list of the steps you need to achieve your goals. Remember, goals can reflect personal growth, like how to be a better person, a better student, a better family member.

TURN DREAMS INTO REALITY

John L. Beckley said, "People don't plan to fail. They fail to plan."

* Spend time thinking about your future / your life.
* Write your goals and dreams in a journal.
* Come up with a plan for achieving your goals.
* Study how people achieve their goals.
* Execute your plan and modify it as you go along.

There are all sorts of self-help books that try to tell you how to achieve your goals. In addition to the generic self-help books, there are self-help gurus who will help you achieve any conceivable goal, from finding your perfect mate to losing weight. However, many of the techniques presented have just been concocted in order to sell books, and in fact actually hamper your success. Richard Wiseman (we mentioned him before) conducted two large studies that followed 5,000 people who were trying to achieve a goal, like quitting smoking, starting a new career, or finding a partner. This is what he found.

TO ACHIEVE A GOAL

Make a step-by-step plan for each part of your goal.

- My goal is to…
- I can achieve this goal because…
- To achieve this goal, I will…
- I will achieve this goal by… Give a specific date.
- My reward will be….
- List 3 benefits of achieving your overall goal
- Go public

Keep in mind your main goal may include several smaller goals (step 2), so for example, if you want to travel to Europe, your step-by-step plan may include 1. Getting a passport, 2. Conning Mom and Dad into paying for the trip, 3. Figuring out where you're going to stay.

33

Learn a Few Inspirational Quotes or Jokes

(Totally not a fluff chapter)

QUOTES

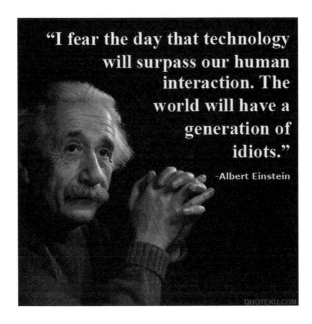

"I fear the day that technology will surpass our human interaction. The world will have a generation of idiots."

-Albert Einstein

QUOTEKU.COM

"If you talk about it, it's a dream; if you envision it, it's possible; but if you schedule it, it's real."

—Tony Robbins

"A great many people believe they are thinking when they are merely rearranging their prejudices."

—William James

"The difference between a dream and a goal is a timeline."

—Dr. Phil

"I taught abnormal psychology for 30 years and could never come up with a definition of abnormal. But a normal person is someone you don't know very well."

—Raymond Moody

"Grant me the serenity to accept the things I cannot change, the courage to change the things I can, and the wisdom to know the difference."

—Alcoholics Anonymous written by Reinhold Niebuhr

(Wondering why we know AA quotes? "Some questions are better left unanswered.")

—Somebody

"You will never be as lazy as whoever named the fireplace."

—Unknown

"You can't believe everything you read online."

—Abraham Lincoln (quote found online)

"People don't plan to fail; they fail to plan."

—John L. Beckley

"Success and failure are often the same thing."

—Dad

Learn a few dad jokes; you never know. How can you tell if it is a dad joke? It's apparent.

Speaking of dads, what did the dad buffalo say when his son left?

Bison.

THREE

HOW TO BE
HEALTHY, WEALTHY,
AND WISE

34

Get Healthy

Having learned how to make thousands of desserts, you may find that you want to consider how to get in shape. Lucky for you, the first step is going to bed. (And if your parents complain about you sleeping until dinner time, you can point to this chapter.)

GO TO BED

Most people, kids included, do not get enough sleep. How can they, when they are forced to stay up late studying the latest video game, or memorizing who ate what on Insta-book (some company names have been changed so we don't get sued), and analyzing the deeper meaning of the photos on Tack-trest? Given our demanding schedules, here are a few pointers about sleep.

Not getting enough sleep makes you stupid. If you are sleep deprived, it is worth reading that again. I did not say, "Not getting enough sleep is stupid." I said that not getting enough sleep makes you stupid. If you don't believe me, the next time you are playing on your phone instead of sleeping, search, "Does lack of sleep make you stupid?"

Not getting enough sleep also affects your mood. Just ask Dad, who clearly needs a nap because he just went ballistic over the small fire I set in the bathtub. (Please note: if your parents are sleep deprived, telling them they need a "nappy poo" does not improve their mood.) Sleep deprivation negatively impacts your immune system and your health. Figure out how much sleep you need. How? Go to bed. When you wake up, see how many hours you slept. Repeat.

The bottom line is that the short-term gains of staying up late have to be balanced against the much larger negative impact sleep deprivation can have on your mood, grades, and health.

Oh, and sleeping late on the weekends will not make up for lost sleep during the week. In fact, depriving yourself of sleep during the week and then trying to catch up on the weekend may compound the problem. It makes sense. If you sleep until two in the afternoon on Sunday and then try to go to bed at a regular time, you will find that you're not tired.

DRINK WATER

How much water do you need to drink? Nobody really knows. Drink when you are thirsty. That said, don't drink bottled water (or water in plastic bottles). Water is water, and you don't need to waste money on "Special Water™." (Unless I can convince my dad to let me sell Special Water™" online.) We're not sure if drinking out of a plastic bottle is a good idea—and it's certainly not good for the environment.

Avoid drinking soda. A 12-ounce can of soda has eight teaspoons of sugar. Caffeinated sodas also have caffeine, which is a diuretic and causes acne. If you like rotting your teeth while sitting on the toilet and getting fat, drink soda. Otherwise, drink water.

A standard 32-ounce bottle of Gatorade has around 14 teaspoons of sugar. Take an empty glass and put 14 teaspoons of sugar in it. Add water. Taste.

Now, if you still want to drink 14 teaspoons of sugar, call your dentist and make an appointment to get dentures.

Avoid pretty much all drinks with sugar. It is hard to advertise blue sugar water to people, so companies slap a label on it that says sports drink or energy drink or vitamin water. Most fruit drinks are no better because they also contain sugar (some almost as much as soda), and they are processed. One apple juice box contains 12 apples worth of sugar.

EAT HEALTHY

On the one hand, America is the land of fat people. Everyone knows that Americans have terrible eating habits and that this causes all sorts of problems. On the other hand, eating disorders are common. Add to this the existence of a multi-billion-dollar diet industry and, well, you can see that we have a problem.

According to Michael Pollan, it isn't hard to eat healthy: "Eat food, not too much, mostly plants." By "food," he means things that your grandma would recognize as food—not Doritos, artificial sugar, "Lunchables," or pretty much any fast food. The rest is self-explanatory. Take a common-sense approach to eating. Grab a healthy snack instead of junk food. Go to a doctor and ask about a healthy diet.

If you want to lose or gain weight, go to a doctor. There is just so much garbage on the internet that it is impossible to discover what is reasonable. In addition, many of the diet programs you read about are businesses intent on selling you stuff. One example is the Atkins diet, a low-carb diet that was popular a few years ago. Basically, people were eating pounds and pounds of meat and avoiding all carbohydrates. Fast-food restaurants got on the bandwagon and offered hamburgers without the bun. When Dr. Atkinson died at the age of 72, the autopsy report showed that he was overweight and had congestive heart failure and hypertension. The lesson of the story is: Get health advice from someone who doesn't profit from the advice they are giving and who knows what they're talking about.

GO TO THE DENTIST

I know what you're thinking. According to the internet, dentists were the ones who invented Halloween to increase business, so they can't be trusted. However, you only get a single set of teeth (sort of) so they're worth taking care of.

If you were not listening to the dentist, the best advice is to brush your teeth and floss. Most dental rinses are useless. When you eat, your mouth produces stuff that helps digest food but that sticks to your teeth. Get this stuff taken off by the dentist twice a year and you probably will not have any cavities.

EXERCISE

Dad claims that "getting up to find the remote" is not exercise. I tried to explain to my dad that the sun can kill me, but he countered that by saying I might die in my sleep. I ended the conversation there. Exercising does more than just help your body. Moderate exercise is as effective as anti-depression medication. Exercise helps improve your mood and helps you sleep and makes you smarter. There are obvious things you can do to get exercise, like going for a run and whatnot, so we will skip those. These are other ideas.

- Join a health club.
- Get a personal plan from a health club.
- Take a Pilates class.
- Join a cycling group.
- Start a walking group.
- Go for a walk with your parents.
- Take your pet for a walk.
- Make your own home gym and charge $80 per person.
- As with diets, find a professional to get advice on creating an exercise program.

AVOID FADS AND UNHEALTHY DIETS

Nobody has the perfect body. In fact, there is no way to define the ideal look because it is different for everyone. That's not to say that people selling you stuff won't try to convince you to look a certain way.

The first step in a healthy diet is understanding your body type. A doctor or nurse can tell you what your healthy weight should be. To maintain a healthy weight, you need to burn as many calories as you eat.

Take time to evaluate your eating habits. Are you eating regular meals? Are you making good choices? Are you skipping meals or loading up on junk food?

Here is the secret—a calorie is a calorie. Diets that focus on avoiding certain types of calories are most likely unhealthy. You will not maintain a healthy weight if you avoid carbs and load up on sugar, so make sure you have a balanced diet. That said, white bread is basically sugar; processed junk food is not really food at all. And some food, like processed lunch meat, is just bad for you

Get a Fitbit or phone app to help track exercise and calories. A 120-pound person burns around 65 calories by walking a mile.

Pills don't work. If they did, nobody would be fat.

MENTAL HEALTH

I'm not a doctor, so my views are personal. I'm amazed by the fact that we talk a lot about our bodies but very little about our brains. It seems to me that our brains are much more complex than, say, our feet. It stands to reason that many more things can go wrong with them.

So, what if something is not quite right with the old noggin? I don't think there is anything to be embarrassed about. Hiding a mental illness is as stupid as not wearing glasses when you need them because you are afraid of what people might think. (Besides, being afraid of what people might think sounds like it might be a phobia or something.)

Whenever Dad is depressed or trying to impress me, he takes me to the pharmacy and walks around the store pointing out things he does not need. "Hey, I don't need adult diapers. Hey, I don't have hemorrhoids, and look, I am not doing any home dentistry... yet."

Since I am not a doctor and really know nothing, I divided mental health signs into two categories: external and internal. External issues are circumstances beyond your control that can hurt you, such as parents getting divorced, the death of a loved one (including a pet), and people who are jerks.

Internal issues are something called feelings. People sometimes feel fat, or ugly or stupid or depressed. The list is endless. But as Alfred

Adler said, "The definition of a normal person is someone who you do not know very well." Being a kid, and in particular a teenager, is an awkward time. Social media certainly does not help because everything that is posted shows people who are looking fabulous while having the time of their lives with equally fabulous friends while we sit at home contemplating our latest pimple and wondering if we have a chance in hell at passing the geometry quiz. We are literally bombarded with unrealistic images of people in situations that are unachievable.

INCOMING DAD RANT—
CONTROVERSY SCORE XXXX

This is why the Kardashians/Jenners dominate the media so much. The Kardashian dad went to OJ Simpson's house to get the murder weapon and then defended that SOB. His kid makes a porn movie and her mom posts it on the internet. Now they have a cult following, a billion-dollar empire, and sell crap at the mall. If that were not bad enough, I am pretty sure they all had plastic surgery. With almost 130 million followers, they can afford to sit around looking marvelous all day while the rest of us spend our days looking for a semi-clean pair of socks, so we are not late for work.

Don't get me wrong, the Kardashian/Jenner group is fine; it's just the photo-shopped unachievable body/lifestyle I oppose. Not only are they projecting an unachievable life, but also an illusion of how they look, of how you could look. They then use these photo-shopped images to sell you stuff so you look like they do, but in fact they don't even look like that. No wonder kids have body image problems!

The best we can do is accept ourselves for who we are and focus on what type of person we want to be. Here's a kind of silly albeit important exercise that helps you to embrace your uniqueness. Take an inventory of yourself and decide what makes you special. Sure, you can obsess over not having a butt the size of a truck or Kim Kardashian's. Or you can take a realistic assessment of yourself and recognize that most of the beauty, health, fashion, and fitness companies use unhealthy models who are photo-shopped into some image of beauty to sell you some product.

UNDERSTAND YOUR BRAIN AND BODY CHEMISTRY

INCOMING DAD RANT— CONTROVERSY SCORE XX

Teenage bodies are like bottles of soda that have been shaken so that when you open them, they explode. This is primarily due to teen hormones (yep, the ones that make hair sprout all over the place). For teenagers, there are occasional bursts of hormones and you may feel odd, moody, tired, etc. Just pay attention to what's happening.

The teenage brain is also growing. Mostly it's growing in the front part of your head. As we already mentioned, your brain is developing and your strong reaction to something may be your five-year-old brain taking over.

Your brain is also kicking out chemicals in the form of hormones. The three big ones are serotonin, melatonin, and dopamine. Melatonin makes you sleepy. Why? Because your brain is growing and like a growing baby you need to sleep. It's like when you have the flu and you have to go to bed. Your body sort of shuts down the non-essential functions and focuses on the issue at hand. For teenagers, the brain is shutting down so it can grow into a more complex brain. Also, your brain is trimming off the connections it has not been using.

The second chemical is dopamine. Dopamine is generated when you do things you enjoy. The thing is, dopamine is actually reduced in the teenage brain, which means you need more of something to create dopamine. This is also related to your brain ignoring risk. Some people believe that as an evolutionary function, having less dopamine and less aversion to risk helped teens leave the cave and start a new life. This makes sense. I can see the teen saying, "Hey, I'm sick of sitting around this cave, I want to explore! That saber-toothed tiger is nothing but a big pussy cat." Understandably, we now say, "Look, my teen needs excitement and is a poor judge of risk. Why don't I let him drive a car?"

The third chemical is serotonin. Serotonin is a chemical that sends signals between your nerve cells. Serotonin impacts every part of your body, including your emotions and motor skills. It helps with sleeping, eating, and digesting, and it helps to regulate emotions and reduces depression and anxiety. This sounds great, but there is a big drawback with this chemical bouncing around. It is not always stable.

Oh, and sex hormones. When someone says a kid is hormonal, well yeah. So why not take some time to read up on what is happening to your body and brain? Pay attention to your mood swings and thought processes. If for whatever reason you find yourself going through severe mood swings, anxiety or depression, ask for help. It's normal. Remember it's normal not to feel normal.

RESOURCES

We may be bending the rules a little by providing links to web pages but here are a few books and web pages that are helpful.

1. Hunger Pains, Mary Piper (When Girls Feel Fat: Helping Girls Though Adolescence)

2. www.kidshealth.org/teen

3. www.about-face.org (deals with body image and media)

4. www.edap.org (eating disorders awareness and prevention)

5. www.loveisrespect.org (Planned Parenthood)

ACTIVITIES

- Create a Health Journal and keep a log of your sleep, exercise, beverages, and food.

- Monitor your junk food.

- Create a plan for getting or staying in shape.

- Develop healthy habits. Don't eat while watching TV or while sitting at the computer. Don't eat in your room or in the car. Don't drink sugar water.

- Go to bed early and learn how much sleep you need.

- Get a watch or phone app and track your exercise

- Make a log of your eating habits to see if you have a balanced diet.

- Remember, most diets do not work.

- Drink water and avoid all other beverages.

- Go to the doctor and dentist for a checkup.

- Know where to get help for you or your friends if there are serious problems such as depression, drug abuse, violence, neglect, physical abuse, or interpersonal issues.

- Read books about the teenage brain and brain chemistry.

- Take an inventory of how the media and social media affects you. Hint: look for magazines with unrealistic standards and people posting pictures that make us feel small. Notice models who are photo-shopped to have unachievable appearances. Even my dad could look halfway decent if we photo-shopped him.

- Talk to your parents about your emotions. Remember the default position for a teenager is often to act like a five-year-old. Help your parents to understand that you're trying to act like an adult (okay, maybe trying to be mature without the full-time job, etc.) but you're still growing.

- Create a healthy lifestyle that works for you. We need healthy eating habits and exercise that is appropriate for our body type.

- Avoid unhealthy habits, especially addictive ones. Your friends may vape or smoke or drink coffee, but you can decide what bad habits to avoid. (Hint: don't waste $4 a day drinking coffee from a shop and skip the $10-a-day nicotine addictions and $100 heroin habit).

35

How to Be Wealthy

"Hey dad, how can I get rich?"

"Easy, do the opposite of what I did."

HOW TO BE POOR

Here are some facts about spending your life in poverty, according to my dad's poverty lectures.

- 12% of Americans are in poverty.
- Of those, 33% are kids, 7% are students, 8% are caregivers, 11% are seniors, 12% are disabled, and 2% are unknown. So only 26% of those in poverty have a job.
- That is pretty good news actually, because if you are not disabled or a retiree, once you finish school your chance of being poor drops to 3.2%.
- Of those with jobs, 33% have part-time jobs by choice, meaning if you work full time the poverty rate drops to 2.1%.

So, stay in school, get a job.

This is worth repeating. If you are a kid and poor, the good news is that you can escape poverty by staying in school and getting a job.

However, it's not quite that easy. There are basically two schools of thought on why people are poor. One is that society is unfair, and people have obstacles that prevent them from escaping poverty. The other is that the very government programs that are intended to help people get out of poverty actually create a system whereby people rely on the government and that keeps them in poverty. With that in mind, over a third of single parents are in poverty; about a third of recent high school dropouts live in poverty.

Therefore, if you want to avoid poverty, stay in school and don't become a single parent.

If you are in poverty, the way out is with a job. That is not to say the world is a level playing field. There are all sorts of factors that contribute to poverty such as race, language skills, where you live, and the quality of education. That said, even if you are poor, you can learn your way out of being poor.

ACTIVITIES

- Think about your financial future.
- Learn the basics of finance.
- How do you calculate a payment if you are paying interest?
- How much money will you have if you save a certain amount each month?
- How much money do you need to save if you want to be a millionaire when you are 35, 45, and 55?
- Learn how to calculate the total cost of an item if you borrow money to buy it.
- Understand the evils of debt.

A PENNY SAVED IS NOT A PENNY EARNED

Ben Franklin must have flunked math class. When you earn a penny, the State and Federal Government want some of your money. Also, the people at the social security office want some. Then there are other government agencies that want some of your money. And in certain states if you spend a penny you need to pay sales tax. Now the tax code is really long and boring but for simplicity's sake, the California sales tax is 10%, and then state and federal taxes take another 25% so a penny saved is 1.35 pennies earned. The obvious lesson is that it is better to save money (or get it from your parents) than to earn money.

Who is wealthy and why? According to Dad, people who dig money out of the ground (such as people with oil, coal, or gold on their property), those who inherit money, movie stars and rock stars, sports heroes, and idiots with reality TV shows. He claims you can get rich by marrying a politician (Senator Dianne Feinstein's husband collected a billion dollars in commissions from selling government-owned post offices). He also claims you can legally steal money by getting a law degree or starting a business.

If you want to make billions, simply buy our book at wholesale prices and sell them for twice the cost. If you want to be a billionaire, simply buy a half a billion dollars' worth of books and sell them for a billion dollars.

"Um Calvin, they would only be half a billionaire."

"Oh right, buy a billion dollars' worth of our books and sell them for two billion."

"No, remember you need to pay taxes."

"Okay, sell 2.35 billion dollars' worth of books."

"Sounds reasonable."

If you are too lazy to sell books you may have to get a job. If that is the case, you could still end up wealthy, if you take the time to learn about money. Since this is a book about things to do, this section includes what you should do to be financially secure.

LEARN BASIC FINANCE

Understanding basic finances is fairly easy. A good place to start is to read *The Richest Man in Babylon*. The book illustrates that the concepts behind saving and investing money have not changed over the past thousand years, and almost anyone can follow the investment strategies. Another great book is *Get a Financial Life* which provides the basics to understand insurance, banking, debt, and investments.

ACTIVITIES

- Read a book or two about money.
- Understand the difference between an asset and a liability. A car is not an asset because it loses value. Your education is an asset because it helps you earn more money.
- Think about how you can do what you love and make a decent living.
- Talk to your parents about money. (This is a great conversation to have the next time they try to talk about sex.)
- Learn the basic concepts of investing. Saving and investing is relatively simple, and the concepts are common sense. Understand risk, (the more risk the higher return, but a greater likelihood of losing your money), diversify (don't put all your eggs in one basket), have a timeline (investments go up and down, so the longer the holding period, the more risk you can

take), understand your risk comfort level, and monitor your investments.

- Open an investment account (as compared to a savings account). Companies such as Charles Schwab will let you open a custodial account with as little as $100. In addition, they will send you a monthly magazine that explains finances.

INCOMING DAD RANT— CONTROVERSY SCORE XXXXX

If one more socialist liberal nut job says that the taxpayers should pay off student debt I will blow a gasket. The average student debt is around $40,000. The average college graduate earns around $700,000 more than a high school graduate. That $40,000 debt is the best money you will ever spend. But why should the taxpayers pay for a student loan when the kids spend the money on beer and hotdogs in Florida over spring break? Why should we pay for some kid to get a useless degree? What's a useless degree? Pretty much any degree that ends with the word studies: Women's Studies, Men's Studies, Gender Studies, Environmental Studies, Social Studies. Any degree that has to add the word science, such as Political Science as opposed to Biology or Chemistry, is also useless. If you are so stupid that you borrow hundreds of thousands of dollars to get some useless degree and then move back into your parents' basement and spend 90% of your take-home pay paying for the beer you drank instead of focusing on a major that would allow you to get a real job, this is your fault.

MOST IMPORTANT FACT ABOUT MONEY

Compound interest is like magic. Basically, if you save money you will earn interest and then you earn interest on the interest and that interest earns interest, and so on. Think of it as the tortoise and the hare race. The tortoise saves a little bit every month, slowly and steadily. The hare tries to do it in one fast sprint at the end.

Imagine two people want to save $100,000 over 25 years. The first person saves $333 a month from the day they turn 20 until they are 45. The second waits until they are 40 and saves $1,667 a month for five years. The person who saves $333 a month will have $441,833 in the bank (if they earn 12% interest on their investments). The person who waits until they turn 40 will have $139,172. Think about it; both people saved $100,000 but one will end up with over three times as much money.

The average person earns around $55,000 a year. At 10% interest, your money can double about every 10 years. So, if you saved 20% of your income, or $916 a month, after 23 years 3 months you will have $1,000,000.

The average car payment hit an all-time high of $550 a month. At 7.5% interest and assuming a new car every five years for 40 years, a person would spend over $1,600,000 on car payments. That same $550 a month invested at 12% will equal $6,369,062.

You don't need to be a financial wizard to be wealthy. You do need a plan and basic understanding about money, investing, and saving.

ACTIVITIES

• Open a brokerage account with $100 at Charles Schwab. The advantage is that they will send you their monthly investment magazine, and if you read through it you will eventually absorb a lot of information about personal finance.

- Okay, you can get finance books, but you can also walk into a bank and talk to an investment advisor.

- Most banks and brokerage firms have basic information about savings and budgets. Most of it is fluff. Look at a site like Charles Schwab; it is a useful site and not too complex.

- Figure out how you can save enough money so that you don't have to always work.

CHAPTER

36

How to Be Happy

"If you want to be happy, study people who are happy."

—Dad

Can money buy you happiness? The old saying is that money cannot buy happiness, but this is only partially true. Studies have shown that having more money does make people happy up to a point. If you make $85,000 a year you cross that threshold, but I guess that would vary depending on where you live, your age, etc. In California or New York, the figure would rise to $125,000. The point is that once you have your basic needs met and a few personal things (perhaps an iPhone), the difference between the iPhone 5 and iPhone 10000005 is very little. Likewise, driving a car may be nicer than taking the bus, but a reliable car is not much different than a luxury car. So why not write down your attitudes about money? Think about the kinds of jobs you could have that would earn the money you need for the lifestyle you want.

In the book, *The Pursuit of Happiness: What makes a Person Happy— and Why?* by David G. Myers, the author reviews a wide range of studies on happiness. Surprisingly, unless you are mentally ill, there are no real criteria for who is happy. Poor people are just as happy as rich people, young people are just as happy as old people, single people are just as happy as married people, and people with kids are just as happy as people without kids.

So, who is happy?

People who decide to be happy. I will repeat that. People who are happy are people who decide to be happy.

If it's true that the people who are happy are those who choose to be happy then why are so many people unhappy? Because they do not know the difference between pleasure and happiness. You can tell the difference because you get sick of things that give you pleasure. For example, if you love ice cream and eat it three times a day, you will eventually get sick of it. It may take a hundred years, but eventually you get bored with anything that gives you pleasure. True happiness is a state of being.

ACTIVITIES

*   What gives you pleasure and what makes you happy?

*   What is the relationship between the things that give you pleasure and happiness? Playing video games may give you pleasure, but any happiness it brings may come from a sense of accomplishment, or from being with friends, or from sharing your experiences.

*   What do you need to be happy? (Hint: Nothing; it's a state of mind.)

*   What can you do to be happy?

*   Now we're kind of going back full circle to the whole media and social media thing. Companies sell things that give you

pleasure. Since most of us would be perfectly happy just being ourselves, they need to "teach you" that you suck. You are ugly, too fat, too thin, too dark, or too light. Your hair is too long, too short, too light, too dark, too straight, or too curly. Your breath will kill a vampire and your clothes make you look like a homeless person.

37

Learn How to Tell if Someone Is Lying to You

One of Dad's favorite mottos is this: Tell the truth, the whole truth and nothing but the truth. You may have heard of it. It's the thing they make you say in court. Dad's been to court quite a few times, you see.

The expression itself identifies the three ways people lie.

"The truth" means not outright lying. If your parents ask you if you did your homework, most kids will not come right out and lie. Instead, most like to skirt the truth.

"The whole truth" means not leaving out key information. If your parents ask you if you did your homework and you say that you finished your math homework but fail to mention that you did not finish your history homework, you have not told the whole truth.

"And nothing but the truth" means you answer the question that was asked. If you say, I did not have much homework today, you have not answered the question.

It's not just people who lie. Organizations lie to the public all the time. Take our good old National Association of Teachers. They state, "Teachers earn a low salary… their salary is in fact lower than those in comparable fields."

It is true that the *starting* salary is low, but the average salary for a teacher is over $58,000, compared to the average income of around $55,000. Their statement is an outright lie.

They also do not tell the whole truth.

Not only does the average teacher earn more than the average person, they work less. The work year for a teacher is around 180 days a year compared with 260 days for everyone else. So even if someone in the private sector earns the same amount per year, a teacher works 1,440 hours, compared with 2,088 hours. In 2018, the average salary for a teacher was $60,483, compared with $61,724, the average salary for someone with a four-year college degree. On an hourly basis, a teacher earns $42.00 per hour, compared with $29.56 for those with a bachelor's degree.

Comparing these salaries is also a lie because they are not telling "Nothing but the Truth" because comparing salaries is not the same as comparing compensation. Salary is only one part of a teacher's compensation. When comparing compensation, that is the total salary and benefits, teachers are raking in the money. In many places a teacher can retire at the age of 55 and collect 60% of their highest year's pay. A teacher earning $75,000 would receive $45,000 plus adjustments for the rest of their life. Since most people cannot collect social security until the age of 65, a teacher will receive almost half a million dollars for not working before a person in the private sector can even think of retiring.

The fact is, a teacher's average salary is only slightly less than those with a four-year college degree. On an hourly basis, a teacher earns over 40% more than those with a bachelor's degree. In addition, teachers can retire 10 years earlier than most people. A teacher who retires at 55 and lives to be 85 will collect over $750,000 more than a person who works to the age of 65 and collects social security after that.

Okay, maybe the rest of the world is underpaid as well....

LIES AND LOGIC FALLACIES

Everyone knows the media is biased. We read two headlines. The first said, "40% of Americans think Trump should sell all of his assets." The second said, "60% of Americans believe Trump should not have to sell his assets." The facts are the same, but one statement is negative, and one is positive.

Or Dad's favorite: "Trump accuses black politician of being a thief." The fact that the politician was black is irrelevant but by adding it to the title it makes it sound as if he is accusing him because he is black. Compare that headline to "Trump accuses politician of being a thief."

So how do we tell if the "news" or "facts" we are reading are credible? We could look at how a genius does it. Not someone who is smart but really smart, like *Guinness Book of World Records* smart.

Marilyn Vos Savant is listed in *The Guinness Book of Records Hall of Fame* as having the highest recorded I.Q.—228. And she wrote a book which may also hold the record for longest title: *The Power of Logical Thinking: Easy Lessons in the Art of Reasoning... and Hard Facts about its Absence in Our Lives Including How Our Own Minds Can Work Against Us, How Numbers and Statistics Can Mislead and How Politicians Exploit Our Innocence.*

The book includes 32 things you can do to improve your critical thinking, but since we ain't that smart, we spent a few days trying to shorten the list and this is what we discovered.

Logic is similar to writing a paragraph. In school we are taught to write a paragraph using P.E.A.R., which stands for:

Point (or Premise)

Evidence

Analysis

Relevance

Let's go back to the teachers' pay argument. You often hear, "Teachers are underpaid. In order to attract better teachers, we should pay teachers more." First of all, teachers are not underpaid; they make as much as other people with bachelor's degrees, work fewer days, and have a great pension. The conclusion that to attract better teachers they need to be paid more is not supported by any evidence. In fact, you could argue that if we paid teachers a billion dollars a year, we would attract people who are interested in money and not in educating kids. We'd also have a lot more teachers. And a lot more debt.

Messed Up Middle (MUM).

Often the statement is correct, and the conclusion is incorrect, because the middle (supporting evidence and analysis) is not evidence or analysis, but another statement.

Here is a simple example of MUM:

Statement: I flunked my math test.

Further statement: My math teacher is terrible.

Conclusion / Implication: It's my teacher's fault I got a poor grade in math.

This simple example shows the statement, which is true, the middle, which is probably not, and the conclusion/ implication, which is definitely not true.

Most examples are not this obvious, but you get the basic idea.

Here is another example: "Oranges are good for you. Orange juice is made from oranges, so orange juice is good for you."

It's not; a glass of orange juice contains 20.83 grams of sugar.

Correlation does not mean causation. Just because two things appear related, that does not mean one causes the other to happen. Superstitions and luck are often attributed to the correlation problem. This example is used in science class all the time: Dihydrogen monoxide is a chemical found in most schools. It is the major component of acid rain, contributes to the "greenhouse effect," may cause severe burns, and in large enough doses it can kill you.

We should ban it from schools, right? Only, it has another name, water.

Politicians are great at mixing up the middle.

Food prices are too high. If we put a price cap on food, prices will not be able to increase.

They did this in Venezuela, and it created hyperinflation because nobody will sell food if they cannot make a profit, so there is now a food shortage. Prices double every two days. (The minimum wage is 250,000 bolivars a month and a dozen eggs cost 480,000 bolivars.)

Advertisers are masters at MUM.

Michael Jackson is a great singer, Michael Jackson drinks Pepsi, and therefore Pepsi must be great. The truth is, Michael Jackson was paid 15 million dollars for commercials for Pepsi. Michael Jackson did not drink Pepsi and would not drink it on the commercials.

WHY STUPID PEOPLE ARE SO SMART

In Dean Burnett's book *Idiot Brain,* there is a section called "Empty vessels make the most noise (Why intelligent people can often lose arguments)." Studies of juries found that confident people are more believable than people with less confidence. Simply put, stupid people are often more confident than smart people. There is actually a name for this: the Dunning-Kruger effect. It was named after a scientist who decided to study stupid people after reading a story about a bank robber who covered his face with lemon juice because lemon juice is used as invisible ink, so he thought his face would not show up on the cameras. The bottom line is, less intelligent people are more confident and simplistic. If you want to come off as smart, act like an idiot.

WHY BELIEFS PERSIST IN THE FACE OF CHANGING INFORMATION

The good news is that young people can be brilliant. Albert Einstein developed the Theory of Relativity when he was 26. There are a number of self-made billionaires who are under the age of 30. There are even kids who have developed new medical procedures. And without going into too much detail, one of the reasons kids are brilliant is that they have an unbridled imagination and are open to new ways of looking at things. In short, they are not hampered by what they already believe to be true.

The bad news is that young people are dumber now than any time in modern history. The high school drop-out rate is over 7%; and more disturbing, almost 20% of high school graduates are functionally illiterate.

In his book *The Art of Thinking Clearly*, Rolf Dobelli summarizes 99 ways in which we make errors in how we think about things. Some of the ideas are fairly common, such as social proof (if everyone believes it, it must be true), confirmation bias (we seek out information that confirms what we already believe), authority bias (believe your teachers because, well they are teachers), and the halo effect. This is when a personality characteristic influences our view. For example, people care what Kim Kardashian thinks because she is a celebrity, despite the fact that she never even went to college. There is also the sleeper effect (we remember facts but not the source), so we believe that a particular product is great, but forget the fact that advertisers told us so.

There are two faults in our logic that appear to be the most important. The first is the Chauffeur Knowledge. This logic error is named after a story about the Nobel Prize winner, Max Planck's chauffeur. Nobel Prize winner Max Planck went on a lecturing tour. His chauffeur got bored with listening to the exact same speech and suggested that they change places. He would give the speech and Max would sit in the audience wearing his hat. The chauffeur gave the speech, but then a physics professor stood up and asked a complicated question. The driver responded by saying, "Never would I have thought that someone from such an advanced city as Munich would ask such a simple question. My chauffeur will answer it."

I love the chauffeur knowledge because a great many people believe they are thinking when they are just regurgitating what others have told them. It is also why I don't believe any news, memes, or social media posts.

The second logic flaw is the overconfidence effect, where we tend to overstate our abilities. This is related to the fact that we trust our own opinions more than those of others. If others disagree with us, they are uninformed, stupid, or know they are wrong but are lying because they have an agenda.

There is one logic flaw that cuts two ways. Our expectations can change our opinions. Teachers who are told certain kids are gifted treat them differently. On the other hand, bigots will view people negatively regardless of their actual abilities. There is a saying attributed to Henry Ford, "Whether you think you can or cannot, you are right", meaning that what is important is your attitude toward the situation.

SMART PEOPLE KNOW THEY ARE DUMB

Okay, trying to be clever here, but do dumb people know they are stupid? The short answer is no, they don't because they lack the cognitive abilities to figure out that they are stupid. At the same time, we already discussed that stupid people may also be over-confident and therefore more convincing.

Smart people have less confidence because they recognize that they don't have all the answers. Heck, they might not even be sure what the question should be. At the same time, intelligent people are more comfortable with ambiguity and know that their beliefs can and will change with new information.

Most people do not like ambiguity. As a result, politicians, teachers, and scientists often make outlandish claims without properly quantifying them or allowing that they may be wrong. Intelligent people understand that most problems are complex and that our opinions may change as we learn more.

But smart people are also better at understanding complex problems and realize that most complex problems require complex solutions. Many of you may have heard of or even read the book *Silent Spring* by Rachel Carson. The book is credited with starting the environment movement when the author, who was not a scientist, convinced people that the rise in childhood cancer was caused by DDT (a pesticide). When DDT was subsequently banned, millions of people actually died. Yes, they died, because it was and is an effective way to kill mosquitoes and stop the spread of malaria. Carson believed that the increase in cancer rates was caused by DDT; but in fact cancer *rates* were level, but bike helmets, car seats, and various medical treatments reduced the *number* of childhood deaths. Thus, it appeared as if cancer *rates* were increasing when in fact the total number of kids who died from cancer remained the same, but the total number of kids who died decreased. By way of example, if 100 kids died and 10 of those died from cancer the cancer rate is 10%; but if only 20 kids died and 10 of those died from cancer the cancer rate increases to 50%. As a result of bad science and mainly due to her book, millions of people died from malaria. Sadly, the book *Silent Spring* is still available.

ACTIVITIES TO MAKE YOU SMARTER

- Practice being able to spot a lie. Is the person or article stating the truth (not a bold-faced lie), the whole truth (not leaving out a key fact), and nothing but the truth (answering the question). Evaluate it this way: Is the statement true? Are the supporting arguments relevant and reasonable? Does the conclusion follow?

- Most jokes are based on the concept that the conclusions do not match the statement, as in this one. "Two idiots were driving to Disneyland. The sign said. "Disneyland left." So they started crying and went home.

- Try making up jokes based on faulty logic.

- Read the news to see if you can spot the logic flaws.

- Read about things you don't agree with (for example, climate change is a hoax) and see if you can find errors or faulty logic in the statement, supporting statements, or facts.

- Read the things that claim the opposite of what you have been told.

- Read books from the opposite end of the political spectrum to yours such as, *Liberty and Tyranny* by Mark Lavin, *How to Talk to a Liberal (If You Must)* by Ann Coulter, *The Savage Nation: Saving America from the Liberal Assault on Our Borders, Language, and Culture* by Dan Savage, or *Giant of the Senate,* by Al Franken .

38

Go on a
Computer Diet

IDR XXXXXXXXXXXX

If you're willing to read a XXXXXXXXXXXX chapter, then you might be one of those teens who look for naughty things on the internet.

Both teens and parents are concerned about how much time teens spend in front of screens, even if the teen may not want to admit it. The average teen spends around 7.5 hours a day in front of a screen, not including doing homework. This section is for teens and parents alike.

This book is not a term paper about the evils of the internet. We're not trying to indoctrinate you—please, fact check us all you'd like. Go to our website. Find your own research and draw your own conclusions. But here's ours. The following is what we've identified as things that we think should concern everybody.

THE BREAKDOWN

Many people will point out problems including social media as a way to compare yourself to others, wasting time, and viewing inappropriate or just plain stupid things.

But viewing inappropriate web pages is not the worst thing. People have been banning books and other sources of information (or entertainment) for decades. In fact, in 1983 the Alabama State Text Book Committed called for banning Anne Frank because it was "a real downer."

Wasting time is not the biggest problem that comes with screen time either. Plenty of people waste time. It's called homework. Just kidding, homework is important; stay in school teens.

Here are the problems we have with the excessive screen time.

WHAT ARE YOU LEARNING?

We think the biggest problem is that the web can turn you into a mindless zombie. Say you decide to get a phone app for your younger sibling, be it out of good intent or spite. We used Google to search for "best apps for infants" and "best video games for toddlers." What we found were people talking about how great games were for their nine-month old kids! One of the most popular games for babies is called Ant Smasher. This is what our Google search showed.

> Ant Smasher – Apps on Google Play
> Rating: 4.1 - 1,195,049 votes - Free - Android - Game
> **Ant** Smasher. Experience this **killer** bug invasion!
> Smash **ants** and bugs with your finger in this great
> game from Best Cool & Fun Games! It's so addictive!

The fact that over a million people voted for this app says something. But think about the game for a minute. There are video games for kids who can't even wipe their own butts. The video games are advertised as being addictive. This is not a warning sign, like on cigarettes, but as a benefit of the game! The game involves killing ants with your finger and losing if you smash a bee. The message seems harmless: don't smash bees—if you don't think about it. Take a moment—it's a game about killing. Yes, you're only killing ants, and it can't be as bad as some of the shoot-em-up games older kids play… right? The underlying message of the game (unintended or not) is that murdering animals is a form of recreation. With little kids, they are incredibly impressionable. Even if you tell them "killing is bad," if they then play a game about killing animals for extended periods of time, the kid is being groomed to become desensitized to death and suffering. If you want to teach your kid that killing is fun, that is your business; but a lot of parents are giving kids the message that this is okay without even knowing it. That's what it really comes down to—unawareness, a lack of mindfulness, a lack of stopping to think— *but what does this actually mean?"*

PHYSICAL PROBLEMS

Scientists took brain scans of kids three to five who spend more than an hour a day looking at a screen and found they had less developed "white matter," an area that is key to the development of language, literacy, and cognitive skills. Cognitive skills are the core skills your brain uses to think, reason, remember, and is required to pay attention.

Finally spending over seven hours a day in front of a screen means you are not exercising. And, well, we probably don't even need to tell you why that's not good.

146

OPPORTUNITY COST

In business there is a concept called "opportunity cost," which is the cost of doing one thing instead of another. The opportunity cost of, say, going to graduate school, is the lost income while in school. The problem with video games and social media is they come at the opportunity cost of doing other, arguable better for college applications, activities. Incels (see below) have lost the opportunity to meet people to date, or have otherwise created unrealistic ideas on partners and dating. Small children playing video games are missing the opportunity to have real interactions, learning opportunities, or the chance to create something neat.

POOR COPING TOOL

On a darker side, people use video games or social medial to escape from problems they face in their life, such as stress from school. But escaping to a video game or chat room doesn't solve the problem. Using drugs, alcohol, video games, or other outlets to run away from a problem (even for a short time) will always make the problem worse. Think of it like a fire or an infection. Trying to drown out your feelings and problems would be a bit like refusing to take antibiotics because then you'd be acknowledging the fact that you're sick, or trying to put out that fire by ignoring it, or pouring some alcohol on it.

CYBER BULLIES

Today teens face bullies on the internet and in person. Young women spend more time on social media than boys, but both post pictures to social media and are subjected to trolls who intentionally post cruel remarks. Not only that, but an embarrassing moment can be filmed and shared with literally hundreds of thousands of people. Teachers report that cyber bullying is common, and teens commit suicide over online comments or shared videos.

We are not psychiatrists, but we think that there have always been bullies and always kids who are ostracized. By picking on one kid, the group of kids feel they belong and are popular. But now people can hide behind their internet persona to harass people. So it's easier than ever for people to harass a person.

But cyberbullying also allows people to become psychotic. People get lost in their online persona and act out their anger and frustration at the world. Happy, well-adjusted people do not go around trolling people. The point is that cyberbullying is a temporary psychosis. (Psychosis is defined as a severe mental disorder in which thought and emotions are so impaired that contact with external reality is lost.) Teens (and adults) are trolling people at the times when people feel the most vulnerable. (I don't want to be patronizing, but teens are growing and changing and learning who they want to be and how to have different relationships. You're bound to have at least a few embarrassing moments.)

The bottom line is that people need to remember perspective. Nothing lasts forever—this certainly won't. Keep in mind your worth is not determined by someone else. While lots of people tell you just to "ignore them," that doesn't always work. Sometimes, standing your ground shows enough confidence that whoever is trying to deal with their pain by bullying you will leave you mostly alone. Regardless, therapy for you and the bully (not necessarily together) might not be a bad idea. When (not if) you are bullied and/or insulted on social media, remember when to stand your ground and when to brush it off. And have compassion for the person who is trying to bully you, because they have unresolved personal issues. A common joking response to mean comments is often "who hurt you?" Remember that. Use it if you want.

In addition, if your social media or gaming partners have dissolved into a continual stream of negative or hurtful comments, it's time for a change.

ARE VIDEO GAMES AND SOCIAL MEDIA REALLY ADDICTING?

The short answer is yes. Playing a video game or being on social media creates dopamine. Dopamine is a chemical your brain produces that makes you feel happy. Take away the dopamine and you can feel bad. More importantly, addictive activities (smoking, gambling, drinking, etc.) remove the work aspect of feeling good. While playing a sports video game and playing a sport both produce dopamine, one is obviously easier. (Some schools now offer Esports instead of going to the gym. I wish I was making that up, but I am not). Physical pain also produces endorphins which are similar to dopamine, but much better if produced from sports like running.

A study from four scientists of the University of Oberta de Catalunya, a university in Spain, analyzed over a hundred studies on video games. In their results, they describe addiction to video games as "an impulse-control disorder with psychological consequences, not unlike other addictive disorders," specifically comparing it to gambling in its neurological "reward system." The study goes on to explain the effects on different parts of the brain, including the dopaminergic system, the pathways involved with producing dopamine.

Translating that into English, they agreed with everything we said.

There are a number of questionnaires on line to determine if you are addicted to media, and most of the questions revolve around the negative consequences of overuse, such as the following:

- "Do you feel guilty?"
- "Do you lie about it?"
- "Do you try to delete games but find new games?"
- "Are your grades suffering?" etc.

TIPS FOR PARENTS

We have spent an insane amount of time thinking about how to address the negative effects of having access to media 24 hours a day. We have concluded that the best approach for both parents and teens is to view screen time the same way we view food. Your goal is to have a healthy diet, whether that is food or computer use.

With little kids, parents have complete control over their diets, and their screen use. With teens however, there's a different dynamic. Teens want more independence, and this can end up causing conflicts with parents who don't want to give up control. On the other end of the spectrum, there are the parents who become neglectful. In reality, there needs to be a balance, both with screen time and the parent-teen relationship. The key to both these? Communication.

Teens need the chance to make mistakes now, when they have the safety net of their family and other resources. If they are prohibited from screens entirely, when there isn't an adult to tell them "no," they're more likely to have a harder time with self-control and addiction. Still, there are ways to guide your teens to that "healthy diet" that even your teens will have trouble complaining about. Here's how:

1. DON'T ENABLE/BE AWARE

Of the kids who play Fortnite, 35% of high school and college kids admitted to skipping school to play. Look up how to tell if your child is addicted to video games or social media; and if turns out to be the case, then parents need to treat game playing like any other addiction. While this may seem drastic, the consequences of spending hundreds of hours in front of a screen can and will adversely affect the child's social and emotional learning and education. The time they are gaming is not spent studying, which can affect the college they can attend or cause the child to flunk out of college, or even high school. Playing games clearly impacts their social life and their ability to learn how to have healthy relationships. Video games are also a passive experience as compared to say, creating a video, which means it is stifling their creativity.

2. TALK WITH YOUR TEENS RATHER THAN NAGGING

There is an old saying, "little kids, little problems; big kids, big problems." With younger kids, it's easy to set rules such as "no screen time on school nights" and "one hour on Saturday after you get your chores done." With teenagers, we are torn between having them discover the consequences of their actions (forget your water bottle or homework, too bad) and setting rules. Too often parents lecture their older teens when one word would suffice such as, "dishes." At the same time, young adults can understand more complex arguments so we want to explain ourselves. So instead of a one-sided lecture, parents need to talk *with* their teens and more importantly listen to their teens. It's easy to tune out a parent droning on about the evils of the internet, but much more difficult to not participate in a discussion about what is appropriate use of a child's time or what they think is appropriate. Setting boundaries with your teens helps them learn to take responsibility for their actions while allowing you, as the parents, to help them.

3. CONTROL TO NEGLECT IN ONE EASY STEP

It's easy for parents to control their young kids; but once they become teens, parents lose a lot of control, simply because their teens have more freedom. At the same time, teens are supposed to differentiate from their parents, and for the lack of a better word, rebel, in order to create their own identity. Unfortunately, many parents simply move from controlling their teens to simply neglecting them. Firm loving parenting with conversations (as compared to lectures) is key.

4. FORGET TEMPORARY SOLUTIONS

Calvin's solution to spending too much time in front of a screen: "Take away their phone, burn the TV, sell their computer online (not sure how to do that without a computer), kick gaming console to the street." Taking away their phones or putting the TV in the garage may be a temporary solution, but it does not address the underlying issue. Teens and many adults need to learn self-control. Teens especially need to develop good lifelong habits. Simply taking away options temporarily will not fix the problem. Taking away a teen's phone is the equivalent of hiding the cookies. It is a temporary solution to a larger problem. Likewise, rewarding teens for good behavior, such as paying them to not use the computer, is a short-term solution that does not address the issue. This is why we compare using the computer to teaching kids how to maintain a healthy diet. Hiding the cookies is not a long-term solution to poor eating habits.

5. BE A GOOD ROLE MODEL

Sitting around binge watching Netflix while nagging your teens to get off their phones does nothing to bolster your argument that they are wasting their time. Likewise, if you are looking at your phone at dinner or while in bed, you can bet your teens will too.

6. IT IS NOT ENOUGH TO TELL THE TEENS TO DO SOMETHING ELSE

Telling your teenager they should go outside instead of wasting their time in front of a screen probably won't do much in the long run. In the short run, your teens may go outside, be bored, and confirm their belief that leaving the house is a bad idea. So rather than randomly sending the teens outside or forcing them off their computers, come up with creative activities with your teens. Better yet, come up with activities to do with your teens. So figure out a list of activities to do with your family. If you need suggestions, there are several lists in this very book for the very purpose.

7. FOCUS ON BIG THINGS

A parent came up to my dad and said, "My son is taking two advanced placement classes, participates in sports, is getting great grades, has great friends, and is studying for the college placement exam. Why should I care if he plays video games?" Our reasoning is simple— who cares? Parents need to set expectations with their teens. While not a complete list, teens should take care of their bodies, take care of their household tasks such as laundry and cleaning the kitchen, get great grades, maintain friendships, have at least one extra-curricular activity, and be forward thinking. They are not expected to be perfect and to keep their rooms neat all the time, but they should be able to clean up before Grandma comes over. If your kids are excelling in the big things, then let some little things slide.

8. DON'T JUDGE (TOO MUCH) / CENSORSHIP

Just because you don't like a game or social media site, that doesn't mean it is terrible. Everybody knows that Instagram images add to a teen's depression, anxiety, negative body image, lower self-esteem, and a host of other problems. But censorship rarely works. In fact, telling a kid not to look at something may add to the appeal. Media always try to push the envelope. There is a huge difference between discussing inappropriate conduct on a show such as South Park, and judging them. Telling a kid you can't believe they waste their time doing something sends a message that there is something wrong with them.

At the same time, if you search "benefits of anorexia," a number of very disturbing sites and chat rooms show up. This is the normal web. It took our dad 29 minutes to get to the "Dark Web" (this includes websites with hidden addresses and users that are difficult to trace). And our dad is "technologically challenged."

Since it is impossible to shelter your teens from information, the best you can do is help them navigate it.

9. TREAT ADDICTION LIKE AN ADDICTION

The negative consequences of using a computer are endless from low self-esteem, suicide, relationship issues, inability to function, dropping out of school, distorted views of men and women, to pure hatred. As we said before using a smartphone produces dopamine which can become addictive. teens get pulled down into a virtual world where they become isolated, lonely and depressed.

Parents need to understand that an addiction to video games, social media or the computer has the same negative impacts as any other addiction. While a person will not overdose from a video game there are children who commit suicide because of cyberbullies. There are also countless teens who commit suicide because of the depression that is related to spending too much time in front of a screen.

TIPS FOR TEENS

1. ARE YOU A MOUSE POTATO?

Obviously if you feel guilty about the time you spend in front of a screen, then you need to find some new activities. If parts of your life are getting neglected, whether it be health, friends, sleep, grades, etc., cut back on your screen time. You get the idea.

2. TAKE THE TTT TEST

Tool, toy, trouble. Are you using screen time as a tool (homework, shopping, weather apps), a toy (social media, gaming, videos) or to get in/cause trouble (bullying, wasting time, inappropriate uses)? Are you using the computer as a toy when you should be using it as a tool? Is your screen time causing trouble in your life?

3. CONTROL, CONTROL, CONTROL

When you were little, your parents controlled your life—what you ate, what you wore, etc. You know how it was. Now, here's a little thing parents don't like to admit. They don't always have all the answers. That doesn't mean you should totally ignore everything they say—they still have a few years of experience on you. But it means that as you grow up, they're still getting the hang of things. Then, just as they're getting used to being able to order you around all the time—boom! Teenagism! Some parents may simply leave you to your devices (figuratively and literally). We like to call this neglect or borderline neglect, but that's the extreme. There are others who refuse to give up control (there's that word again) or struggle to treat you as if you're not five. Now, we can't account for all parents, but it's likely you've disagreed with them at some point in your teenage years (or will). What makes it really hard for parents to argue with you is when you approach things in a mature way. This means talking to them politely, or apologizing when your gut reaction gets the better of you. If you communicate your desires and act like an adult (even when your parents don't), it's a lot harder for them to treat you like you're five. In the end, taking responsibility is the surest way to gain control—of your life, your health, and your time.

4. MINDFUL SCREEN TIME

Unlike almost any other vice, our smartphones are with us constantly. Even smokers have to take a break in the shower, yet we can listen to podcasts no matter where we are. Being mindful means making a decision as to what you are doing with your screen time, rather than looking at your phone as a default, or simply playing a video game or watching a video whenever you have free time. You know those times when you check your phone, and when you look up, you realize you've been watching seven hours of cat videos and you can't remember how you even got there? That's where the mindfulness comes in. It's hard, but it is a skill everybody young and old needs to learn.

INCOMING DAD RANT X
(DAD RANT WITHIN A DAD RANT, WE KNOW)

OKAY BOOMER

Yep, the old people always kvetch about the young generation. I am sure "Thog the caveman" complained that his teens spent all of their time inside the cave drawing on the cave wall, making some kind of circular rolling thing, instead of sitting around the fire with the family.

Smartphones provide instant entertainment but it is shallow. There is a huge difference between watching a romantic comedy and falling in love. Spending over a hundred days a year looking at a screen is not only a colossal waste of time, but it is ultimately an empty, depressing, and isolating habit. The isolation is now so pervasive that there are terms to describe the lack of connection. The term "involuntary celibate" (shortened to "incel") refers to self-identifying members of an online subculture based around the inability to find a romantic partner, despite desiring one.

The isolation is both physical and emotional. Simply filling your time with mindless activities does not make you happy. Happiness comes from inside. You can choose to be happy. Watching TV may be enjoyable for a time, but it does not lead to a sense of purpose, fulfillment, and happiness.

Our webpage is called the Mindful Cynic, because it is one thing to say that we should be mindful of our activities and live in the moment, and another thing to actually be mindful while sitting in class. So the cynical dad chimes in and points out that both kids and adults can find themselves wasting hours in front of a screen.

I like using the diet analogy to explain screen time. As a teen, your parents don't have as much control over your diet so it's up to you to maintain a healthy diet. How do you maintain a healthy diet? You chose to. We call it mindfulness, but basically if you want to maintain a healthy diet, then you need to pay attention to what you are eating. It is a never-ending balancing act. Sure, you may have some junk food, but overall you want to eat a healthy balanced diet. Likewise, you may periodically binge-watch a special Netflix show, but don't spend five hours a day on mindlessly following superstars or playing a game. Fast food may taste good, but that does not mean it is good for you. Being temporarily entertained is not the same as being fulfilled.

A slight digression (it will all make sense; trust me): I have a friend who is a terrible cook. I mean really terrible. At one dinner party she used a cup of salt instead of a teaspoon rendering her dinner completely inedible. At another party, guests tried to guess if they were eating fish, ham, or chicken (it tasted like dish soap). She also lacks basic kitchen wares, and so you may find yourself eating pasta off of a Frisbee with a serving spoon or drinking out of a soup bowl. Despite her clear limitations, she has great dinner parties. The reason she does not have enough silverware is that nobody turns down her invitations, and guests often bring uninvited friends, which is fine by her. My point is that there are a lot of cooking shows, but those will fade from your memory; but it is unlikely that I will forget a dinner party where the hosts asked if I could bring seven jars of pickles, a can of tuna, and some grapes.

In the end, it's up to you what you do with your life. You can decide to be mindful, to spend ten minutes in the morning deciding why today is a good day to take chances and try to live a life worth talking about. Or to sit in front of a screen for the majority of your life. And if you find you are bored because you are not on a device, remember that creativity, innovation, art, music, inventions, and dreams are all born out of boredom (or desire for money, take your pick).

39

Self Discovery and Conscious Living

RELIGION

There is an old saying. "Never discuss religion or politics" so let's do both and try not to offend anyone. I have friends who are Christians, Jews, Muslims, Mormons, and Atheists. It never occurred to me that it may be helpful to have a general understanding of what they (or their families) believe. I think at a minimum everyone should at least have a basic understanding of the top six religions. Why? Because it is estimated that there are over two billion Christians, over a billion Muslims, over a billion non-religious people, and over a billion people practicing Hinduism, Chinese Folk Religion, and Buddhism. Altogether, that is over 5 billion people, so there is a good chance that you will meet people who practice these religions. In addition, while we claim to have a separation of church and state, the fact is that politics and political strife is often intertwined with religion.

Our suggestion for learning about the most popular religions include:

- Learn about Christianity
- Learn about Islam
- Learn about Judaism
- Learn about Hinduism
- Learn about Chinese Folk Religion

ACTIVITIES

- If you have friends who are religious, ask them about their religion.
- Read books about various religions.
- Beware of anyone one who makes vague promises about enlightenment (think cult).
- Recognize that every religion has its good ideas and bad, as well as fables and myths. (The story of Noah's Ark, or the idea that the only guaranteed way into heaven is by killing infidels.)
- An unevolved view of religion dismisses the spiritual aspects because the stories may clash with science. An evolved view considers the religion in relationship to the individual and culture.

MINDFULNESS

Some of us dislike the word "spiritual" as it conjures up images of self-righteous vegans who smell of incense, wear flip flops, speak in a half-whisper, bow, and say "Namaste" (which means I bow to the god within you). However, there is value in an inward spiritual path. So here we are summarizing the basic tenets of Buddhism. It's also a good template for researching a religion.

1. Life is full of dukkha.

Dukkha is usually defined as suffering, but it also means disappointment, frustration, or grief.

Even if things are okay at the moment, they won't always be great. We all go through painful and frustrating moments.

2. Suffering (dukkha) has a cause.

The cause is our attachment to the familiar, the known. It is our "desire."

3. The cause of suffering can be ended by releasing expectations and attachments.

We can still have meaningful relationships but without that needy, clingy attachment based on fear of loss and fear of being alone, fear of the unknown.

4. Meditation, or the practice of mindfulness and awareness, is the way to end suffering. We try to focus on the present. The meditations also focus on the Eightfold path. As you might have guessed, there are eight ideas in the path.

1. The right view or way of perceiving the world: See things without expectation, judgment, or preconceived notions. See things as they are.

2. The right intention: Work from a place of pure intentions (try not to harm anyone or anything). No manipulating.

3. The right speech: Say what you need to say and say it from the heart.

4. The right discipline: Give up your tendency to complicate things by imposing your expectations of how things should be.

5. The right life: "Bloom where you're planted" or do your personal best no matter the situation.

6. The right effort: Do things the right way.

7. The right mindfulness: You become mindful of the most minute, mundane, tiny details of your life experience, such as the way you talk, the way you stand, the way you walk, your thoughts, your emotions, the way you study, the way you work, how you treat people.

8. The right concentration: Most of the time, we run on autopilot. Meditation allows you to discipline your mind to remain present.

INCOMING DAD RANT— CONTROVERSY XX

People have taken the five-thousand-year-old practice of yoga and turned it into a way to sell tight pants to rich white women. Not to mention that pretty much anyone can call themselves a yogi. I am surprised Kim Kardashian has not started a line of yoga. (Oh, it turns out that Kim did "naked yoga" on her TV show.) My point is that reading the Ten Commandments does not make you a Christian, and taking a Saturday morning yoga class does not make you enlightened. Yoga is not slow-moving aerobics, and a spiritual practice is a practice that helps you to evolve.

ACTIVITIES

- Take a yoga class.
- Go to the library and check out a book on meditation.
- Learn how to meditate.
- Learn about Buddhism or other meditative practices.
- Take the time to explore your own spiritual path.

40

Book Suggestions

YOUNG ADULT, AND CHILDREN

We thought about putting a list of our favorite books here, but then we remembered that there is a place called a library where there are thousands of books for free.

41

We Need Your Help

If you want to get rich, quick go to our website mindfulcynic.com page and click the link that says *get rich quick*. Here you can buy our books at a discount and sell them to your friends and family and make a huge profit.

Click on our website. Send us your ideas for things to do. We won't give you credit if we steal your idea, but they say that helping others is its own reward. Or something like that.

About the Authors

We live in California with our two cats, though Dad was originally from Wisconsin.

Ironically, this book was written on the computer.

Here are some more specific blurbs:

 **Studious Student Daughter, aka Alexandra Boyden Walker.** (I put my real name so I can get credit for the book and satisfy the whole "using it for college thing.") Most of my work involved cutting out Dad's rants, and damnation, there were a lot of them. I'll probably be ~~fourteen~~ thirty by the time this book gets published.

You should totally vote for her.

 **Dad, aka "the old man."** If I had to explain what he does, I'd say complaining and avoiding work. Mostly though, he comes out of his office to pet the cats or tell us he is going to take a shower and delay the inevitable. He tends to become invested in something and then do a ton of research followed by a ton of lectures on said subject. Suffice it to say, there were a lot more of his rants in the first draft. Though he probably won't admit it (he's

trying to use this book to get us into college, apparently), he actually had quite a hand in making this book possible, including research, production, writing, and threats.

 **Brother, aka Calvin Boyden Walker.** This book really did start with my dad making me write a list of 1,000 things to do without a computer as punishment for spending too much time on the computer. Of course, my list included: wake up, get out of bed, put on one sock, put on second sock, put on third sock, etc. Then my dad started dropping piles of books on my bed with instructions on how I was to find new activities. Hopefully by the time you read this I will no longer be in 10th grade. Although if my dad keeps making me work on this book, I may not have enough time to study and flunk out. My hobbies include playing video games on my computer, playing video games on my phone, having friends come over to play video games, going to my friend's house to play video games and thinking about playing video games while running in track. I attend a Charter School where I study digital art (how to make video games).

Mom, aka Genevieve Walker, wants to make sure that we mention she had nothing to do with this book as she doesn't want to be sued or associated with it and Dad's ramblings. (I cut out most of them.) She is also a school teacher.

By the way, if you do want to sue us for plagiarism, Dad, aka **Paul J. Walker**, wrote this book all by himself.

You can reach all of us at www.Mindfulcynic.com

Works Cited

Bauerlein, Mark. *The Dumbest Generation: How the Digital Age Stupefies Young Americans and Jeopardizes Our Future: or, Don't Trust Anyone under 30.* Jeremy P. Tarcher/Penguin, 2009.

Berens, Linda V., and Dario Nardi. *The 16 Sixteen Personality Types: Descriptions for Self-Discovery.* Telos Pub., 1999.

"Better Information. Better Health." WebMD, WebMD, webmd.com/.

Clason, George S. *The Richest Man in Babylon: Illustrated.* BN Pub., 2007.

Houston, Philip. *Spy the Lie: Former CIA Officers Show You How to Detect Deception.* St. Martin's Press, 2012.

Burnett, Dean. *The Idiot Brain: a Neuroscientist Explains What Your Head Is Really up To.* Guardian Faber, 2017.

Kiyosaki, Robert T. *Rich Dad, Poor Dad.* Recorded Books, 2001.

Koppel, Ted. *Lights out: a Cyberattack, a Nation Unprepared, Surviving the Aftermath.* Crown Publishers, 2015.

Myers, David G. *The Pursuit of Happiness: Who Is Happy —and Why.* Aquarian/Thorsons, 1993.

Palaus, Marc, et al. "Neural Basis of Video Gaming: A Systematic Review." *Frontiers in Human Neuroscience,* vol. 11, 2017, doi:10.3389/fnhum.2017.00248.

Radin, Dean. *Entangled Minds: Extrasensory Experiences in a Quantum Reality.* Paraview, 2006.

Radin, Dean I. *Real Magic: Ancient Wisdom, Modern Science, and a Guide to the Secret Power of the Universe.* Harmony Books, 2018.

Radin, Dean. *Supernormal.* Crown Publishing Group, 2013.

Radin, Dean I. *The Conscious Universe: The Scientific Truth of Psychic Phenomena.* HarperOne, 2009.

Ramsey, Dave. *Foundations in Personal Finance.* Lampo Group, 2014.

Ramsey, Dave. *The Money Answer Book: Quick Answers to Everyday Financial Questions.* Thomas Nelson, 2010.

Stanley, Thomas J., and William D. Danko. *The Millionaire Next Door: The Surprising Secrets of America's Wealthy.* Pocket Books, 1996.

Tobias, Andrew P. *The Only Investment Guide You'll Ever Need.* Mariner Books, Houghton Mifflin Harcourt, 2016.